May we all be blessed.

With blessings + love
Donna Mieskal

Insights

Inspiration for Daily Living

With a Special Section on Moving Through Grief

DONNA HUBER MIESBACH

enspiritus
publications

Insights: Inspiration for Daily Living

©2022 *Donna Huber Miesbach*

A word of deep gratitude to Nilgirl Press for permission to relate the stories about Gandhi and Badshah Khan, as found in Eknath Easwaran's books, *Gandhi, the Man* and *Badshah Khan, Nonviolent Soldier of Islam.*

Design by Enspiritus Publications

Early Consultants - Mahaila McKellar & Lissa Coffey

Editing by Donna Miesbach

Proofing by Valarie Palacios

Cover photo of the Backwaters in Kerala, India, taken by the author

Paperback: 978-0-9859318-3-4

Kindle: 978-0-9859318-4-1

Library of Congress Control Number: 2022906367

Cataloging in Publication Data on file with publisher.

Additional copies of *Insights* are available through amazon.com.

For information on the author, please go to www. donnamiesbach.com.

Questions may be directed to dmiesbach@cox.net.

Printed in the United States of America

10 9 8 7 6 5 4 3 2 1

Praise for Insights

"I have always enjoyed reading Donna's words of wisdom over the years and am delighted that she is now offering them in this compilation. Whether you choose to start at the beginning and read them systematically or randomly turn to one, the message contained in each, will awaken your soul, lighten your step and inspire your journey through life."

Roger Gabriel
Chopra Global Chief Meditation Officer

"Beautifully written, honoring timeless wisdom and teachings, Donna brings to our attention her interpretations of life experiences that we all share. Open the book and let the words remind you to breathe, to slow down, to love, to be kind to yourself, and to experience all the lowest and highest moments with love, strength and encouragement. A daily read with a wonderful guide."

Leanne Backer Fenton
Former Chopra Center Executive Chef, now retired and playing

"Donna Miesbach has been a colleague for more than 20 years. She is as sweet, generous and kind as she is strong, insightful and wise. Donna has the ability to take ancient teachings, combine them with her vast life experience and convey the resultant synthesis in a way that speaks to one's soul. She has been writing her pearls of wisdom on a weekly basis for many years. Now she has compiled the best into a book that we'll all want to have close at hand."

Mahaila McKellar
Certified Chopra Global Meditation Instructor since 1998. Her continued studies took her to Tulum, Sri Lanka, and Osho's ashram in Pune, India. Great educators she has studied with include Dr. Deepak Chopra, David Daniel Kennedy, Debbie Ford, Tony Robbins, Roger Gabriel, and Dr. David Simon.

"Donna Miesbach's latest book speaks to the heart of who we really are. How she integrates the wisdom gained from her own experiences with principles from today's leading teachers is powerful. To have been able to ponder on her 'Thought for the Week' series and her insightful journey with grief these many years has been a blessing. Putting her work in one book is truly a gift of Unconditional Love. Thank you, Donna!"

Dr. Tommie Radd
Full Professor of Counselor Education, Retired
Founder of the "Grow with Guidance" program (see www.allsucceed.com)
The Dr. Tommie Radd Professorship in School Counselor Education, Ohio University

"This beautiful book contains a treasure of Insights on how to effectively respond to today's life challenges. Written for all ages and stages of life, Donna Miesbach's messages are especially relevant during these turbulent times.

"The guidance offered in this book covers a wide range of human experience. In her own gentle way, Donna couples her own personal experiences with the wisdom of ancient scriptures and today's renowned authors and leaders in the mind-body field. Drawn from her 'Thought for the Week' series, the Insights she offers from Gandhi, Dr. Deepak Chopra, Dr. Jon Kabat-Zinn, Osho, Dr. David Hawkins, Dr. Bernie Siegel, Sri Ramana Maharshi, Thich Nhat Hahn, Brother Lawrence, and many others, add to the richness of this collection.

"Whether you are dealing with Grief, Adversity or Change, this profound book will give you a fresh perspective on your journey through life."

Joanne Scanlon
Reiki Master, Hospice CNA
Certified Chopra Global Meditation Instructor
Mindfulness-Based Stress Reduction Professional

"Here is a backpack of spiritual snacks that will help you refuel and reorient your journey through life. Profound, yet simple. A deep well that is overflowing with inspiration. It's valuable for a weekly practice of guided reflection, as well as spontaneous quick reference by topic. Truly a treasure chest of wisdom, insight and grace. It reminds me of Khalil Gibran's *The Prophet*.

Ryan Palmer
B. A., LREP, Consultant, Advocate, Writer, Farmer, Permaculturist

"Here is a collection of Insights containing whimsy, kindness, and most of all love. Love for self, love for others, and love for our planet. I have had the honor of being in Donna's calming presence on many occasions. Through these writings I believe you will feel her calming presence, too, and gain inspiration for daily living. Treat yourself to the wisdom she shares. Then treat someone you love to this timeless collection."

Gabrielle Van Houten
Ayurvedic Health Practitioner
Chopra Total Wellbeing Coach

"Many years ago, I traveled to Omaha for a March weekend of one-on-one instruction in Chopra's primordial sound meditation with Donna Miesbach. Little did I know Donna's instruction, wisdom and kindness would impact the arc of my life in profound ways, beginning with the practice of tuning in daily to the stillness and peace within myself. Her 'Thought for the Week' messages are 'drops of wisdom,' bread crumbs of learning along the trail of life. Now, in *Insights: Inspiration for Daily Living*, you, too, can follow her sign posts to living your life with purpose, intention and resiliency."

John Norwood
John is a lifelong learner, drawing inspiration from the extraordinary to the mundane. A mission-driven professional devoted to public service and a purpose-driven life.

"The years 2014 through 2018 in my work life were especially challenging, which in turn had a big impact on my life in general. I came upon Donna's writing in 2018 through reading the Daily Word from Unity Church. I was definitely seeking during that time. I have always found great comfort and usually very practical advice from reading or listening to what I would describe as 'spiritual' publications, so I did a little searching about Donna and her writings and BINGO, I really found a goldmine!Her short and thoughtful 'Thought for the Week' messages were a sort of life line for me at that time, and still are. When her weekly emails arrive, I am still amazed how 'right on target' for me that particular message is on that particular day or that week. What I most love and appreciate about her writings is the encouragement I always receive. They make me think "I feel that way too," and "I really do have the tools to make the changes I want to make." It just takes practice and never giving up on myself or others.

"Donna's encouragement to not give up and love myself has helped me make great progress on my life journey. Now that I have entered retirement after 31 years, I am seeking more than ever for wisdom and guidance. I know I will hardly ever 'get it right the first time' but I also know her love and wisdom will encourage me to keep moving onward and upward. Thank you for sharing your wealth of readings and insights with us."

Gail Gentry
Retired Institutional Researcher, Austin College

"I found this book to be full of new insights and perspectives, guide lines for navigating life's challenges, and the joy and freedom of inspired thought. All written in clear and concise language. A wonderful, refreshing read for us all."

Jean Johnson
Retired Educator

Other Books & Publications by Donna Miesbach

Gleanings – A Bi-Monthly Discussion of Life Issues™ 1996-2004

Tools for Teens: A Course in Life Skills for People on the Growing Edge 2000

Thought for the Week Series 2001 to present

Trails of Stardust, Poems of Inspiration and Insight 2002

From Grief to Joy, A Journey Back to Life & Living 2012

Moving Through Grief: A Guide to Inner Wholeness 2015

A Few Spontaneous Poems 2021

Honors

Inspirational Poet of the Year 1985, awarded by *The Poet Magazine*

Silver Nautilus Award 2012, from the Nautilus Book Awards Foundation

Books with Coach Greg Roeszler via Playmakers Press

Coaching for a Bigger Win: A Playbook for Coaches 2009

Coaching Character and Leadership: A Playbook for Parents 2017

Beyond Coaching: Building Character and Leadership 2020

Never Ending Season: Diary of an Inner City Coach (available in 2022)

Contents

Year Two

Year Three

Year Four

Moving Through Grief

With Deep Appreciation
To All of My Teachers,
Including Life Itself

To Our Readers

Soon after my husband's sudden passing in 1994, I learned about Dr. Deepak Chopra and his courses on meditation, holistic living and yoga. The timing was perfect, as I very much needed to restore meaning and purpose to my life, and so it was that a new journey began.

What I learned made such a difference in my life that I committed to becoming certified to teach both meditation and yoga. That opened the door to meeting—and teaching—many people who quickly became friends.

As the years went by, other doors opened that allowed me to study with other teachers, too. The composite of these teachings was so rich, I felt compelled to share these Insights with my students through a "Thought for the Week" series.

Now here I am with nearly 25 years of Thoughts that have gone out. As I was looking through them recently, it occurred to me that this storehouse of Insights could be shared with others who are also trying to find their way. This collection is the result of that musing.

Please feel free to browse through this book and read it as your Spirit moves you. There are over 200 entries, set up in a 4-year format, along with a special section on "Moving Through Grief."

Let these Thoughts resonate within you. Ponder them. Go deep inside and see what your heart is saying. That is where your deepest truth resides.

Trust what your heart tells you. Let it be your guide. It is your surest voice.

With blessings and love,

Donna

Year One

Week 1. You Are Never Lost

God is the Master Designer. When I look back at the past 27 years, I am amazed at how the pieces fell in place. One by one, a new life and a new way of being took shape. It was so subtle, I didn't recognize at the time that something new—even something profound—was taking shape, and yet it was. Each step was like a revelation—something I hadn't thought of before but which I welcomed with open arms when it came. It was as though what I had always wanted was being given in ways I could never have thought of myself.

In looking back, it seems to me there must have been a Master Plan that was in place all along. The mystery of it, the wonder of it, and yes, the beauty of it, still leaves me in awe. Certainly I couldn't see this when I was going through the loss of my husband and both parents, one right after the other.

What I have found is that life is always moving us toward new heights. And this is true for all of us! When you truly understand this, you also know that you are never lost, even though it may seem so. There is an uplifting energy that is always at work in your life.

Some call it God. Others call it Love.

Week 2. Tuning In

Have you ever noticed how deeply you are at peace when your mind is absolutely quiet?

That peace is you.

Have you ever noticed the stillness that is at the center of that peace?

That stillness is also you.

Stillness and peace are the very essence of your soul.

That peace and that silence are always here because you are always here.

All it takes is a shift of attention, a tuning in, and there you are. And there it is.

There is no difference.

Week 3. Doing and Becoming

When we truly believe something, it becomes the standard by which we live our life.

If we live by that standard, eventually there will be no difference between what we believe and what we are. Our actions, thoughts and feelings will all reflect what we have become. It just naturally follows that what we have become is what we have believed.

It's always like that, isn't it?

So what is it that you truly believe?

Is that how you are living your life?

The only way to become what you believe—at least as I see it—is to put that principle into action through practice, and more practice.

It is in the doing that we become.

Week 4. Trust

While there may be times when it may not seem so, your life really is moving in harmony with a rhythm that is not of your making.

What does this mean? Well, it means that your life is unfolding according to a Wisdom that is beyond your understanding.

Then what is your part? To be open to this leading. Seek always to follow the Higher Will. Grace knows the way and is your infallible Guide.

Whether it may seem so or not, you can never really be lost, so trust in that Higher Wisdom and know that the universe itself is working on your behalf. Of that we can be certain. Why? Because That which is guiding the planets and stars of this immeasurable universe is also guiding you.

Week 5. There Will Always Be Change

Being open to the lessons inherent in our challenges is a very productive approach. We change as we mature and learn from our experiences. Being flexible and open to new ways of doing things, and yes, new ways of being, makes a huge difference.

Where we are mentally and emotionally at any point in time isn't set forever. It's just where we are on our own personal scale of growth. Learning to be a Responsible Choice Maker is key. Will the choice we are considering have the results we desire? Will it bless us? Will it bless others? Will it keep us moving in the best possible direction?

Whether we like it or not, there will always be change. Learning to go with the flow brings inner stability and balance, even in the midst of chaos.

Eventually, we begin to understand that inwardly we are all right, regardless of what else is going on. There may be times when we need a lot of help outwardly, but when we know our soul is intact and we are okay, navigating through the waters of life becomes much easier.

Week 6. That Silent Inner Calling

There are those on this planet who seem to be following an invisible drummer. They don't know where that inaudible music will take them, but in their hearts they know that wherever that leading does take them, that is where they long to go.

Somehow these souls have sensed that there is far more than what the eye can see, even beyond what the mind can imagine. It is That toward which they are being drawn, and it is That which is calling them to Itself.

This is true for all of us. Once this potential awakens within us, nothing else can satisfy the hunger—even the longing—it creates within us. When that time does come, all we can do is follow its leading, for this unfolding is not just of our own doing. It is part of something larger—much larger—that is at work within us.

That inexpressible dynamic comes from the very root of our being. To hear and follow our silent inner calling changes everything. Wisdom far beyond the scope of common understanding begins revealing itself in ways unknown before. We see with new eyes and begin hearing our own heart's deep messages. It is a voice unlike any other. We long to heed its call, for its leading is sure, its promise is immense. Who could ask for more than that?

Week 7. Hitting the Wall

Have you ever felt stuck when you were working on something? I know I have. All of a sudden you hit a wall and can't go any farther.

Apparently that has happened to Dr. Deepak Chopra, too, because he says when things don't go his way, he lets go and trusts that a Higher Wisdom is at work.

It's interesting the difference this approach makes. Opening yourself to that Higher Wisdom gets you out of the way and allows things to flow. Instead of trying to force something, when you're aligned with God's timing, things just come together in unexpected ways.

Whenever you get stuck and can't find any answers, try letting go and see what happens.

Week 8. Growing Younger

Did you know your body can improve with age? Yes, I'm reading Deepak's *Ageless Body, Timeless Mind*, and it has captured my attention. Why? Because Deepak is saying that life is a process of constant transformation and therefore is full of potential and unlimited growth. More than that, you can choose to meet life with joy, creativity and curiosity!

According to Deepak, automatic decline is not programmed into our bodies! Instead, issues of the mind and heart actually determine, to a very large extent, the quality of our aging. He says that even simple things like breath work and attention can undo long term symptoms to a very large extent.

That certainly gave me pause for thought! How about you?

Week 9. A Confession

Slipping into our old ways of thinking can happen without our even knowing it. Just the other day, when things got pretty complicated, I heard myself repeating, "This is so hard!" The more I held that thought, the harder it became.

Then, when I sat down to do some afternoon reading, what do you suppose I came across? A passage where Deepak tells us that we have to look beyond our interpretations so a different reality can shine through. If we can learn to do this, eventually we do find that deeper place where everything is all right. (*Ageless Body, Timeless Mind*)

Before I knew it, I was laughing at myself, at the situation, at allowing myself to slip into that old groove.

I've known for quite a while that nothing and no one can hurt you without your permission (Thank you, Eleanor Roosevelt!), but when I was feeling overwhelmed, that old record started playing again.

The key is remembering to pay attention. To live our lives with awareness and not take things so seriously. It's a practice. For all of us. So how about it? I will if you will…

Week 10. Being at Peace

Years ago an author I came across compared life to being on a raft. He said if you wanted smooth sailing, you had to keep the turbulent water from spilling over into your boat. The turbulent water would be the waves of anger and frustration that make for rough sailing. That was my introduction to conscious choice making. While that new perspective was helpful, it took me a while to understand that being at peace is totally an inside job.

Emmett Fox says you can have your indignation or you can have peace, but you cannot have both. That is why you need to develop a relationship with the part of yourself where peace resides. When you do begin to experience that peace, you have touched upon the very essence and core of your being. That Changes Everything.

I say that because the more you open yourself to deep inner peace, the more the memory of it stays with you and the easier it becomes to remain at peace when you find yourself in heavy seas.

You can do that because every day you are setting your anchor in the sacred Presence that always carries you through, regardless. When that Presence is your foundation, a new way of meeting life opens for you, and you are blessed indeed.

Week 11. Conscious Living

Have you ever had two voices going on inside you? One says this and the other says that? I know I have. But how to choose?

Author Gary Zukav says when those times come, think of it as though you are looking at a road map. Each of the options will take you in a specific direction. That being so, what would be the consequences of each option? Which one will bring you the results you are seeking? He says inner conflict is really a gift! You are being given the opportunity to choose before you act, instead of acting rashly or without forethought and ending up where you don't want to be.

Zukav calls this conscious living. It begins with being aware, with paying attention and making conscious choices. When those times come, and they do for all of us, ask yourself which choice will bless you and others, too? Which one will bring peace to your spirit? Which one will keep you on the higher road?

Any time we choose the higher road, enormous support is there to help us, to gird us up, to strengthen and encourage us. We never have to do these things alone, but we do have to make that conscious choice.

The beautiful part about this is—each time we deliberately live our life consciously, it gets easier. We are learning to let our heart lead us. The heart is always wiser than the head. When we listen to our heart, we open ourselves to our soul's wisdom. When we follow that leading, the Love and Wisdom that have always been within us become a natural part of our expression.

Week 12. A Life Well Lived

Deepak's book, *Ageless Body, Timeless Mind,* got me started on this journey back in 1996. While I never could have said it the way Deepak does, it seemed like pure logic from the very first reading. I've read it several times since, and continue to learn from it even now. Today I'd like to share Deepak's view about the mind/body connection and how we influence that connection both consciously and unconsciously.

To begin with, Deepak reminds us that our cells literally metabolize our personal views, which means our body mirrors our silent, inner attitudes. For that mirroring to be what we want it to be, we must be aware of our responses instead of living our life on automatic.

When we are aware, we actively influence our body's inner activity through conscious choice making. That is possible because every cell knows what we are thinking and feeling all of the time!

If we are depressed, the body's systems are depressed, too. If we are angry or upset, that emotional inflammation disrupts our body's harmonious functions. In other words, the body's efficiency is at the mercy of our attitudes—all of the time! I find that pretty amazing.

The key is conscious choice making. We do that by paying attention, and why wouldn't we? After all, a conscious life is a life well lived, challenges and all.

Week 13. One Basic Lesson

Dr. David Hawkins tells us there is one basic lesson underneath life's many challenges. That one lesson resolves all other lessons and restores peace and harmony in our heart and in our life.

What could that one basic lesson possibly be? What is so powerful that it raises us up above all the things which tend to pull us down?

No doubt we each have our own answer to that question. As I see it, the answer is Unconditional Love. When Love replaces judgment with acceptance, it transforms criticism into compassion.

When our negative tendencies have been cleansed from our psyche, what remains is joy and peace and the unconditional love that makes it all possible.

Learning to love at this deep level transforms us, our relationships, our circumstances, and thus our lives. Easy to say but hard to do? Indeed it is. As with all things, life is a practice.

What could be more important than learning to truly love and accept each other?

Week 14. Three Important Keys

If ever you've wondered how to be calm and centered when discord confronts you, Dr. David Hawkins offers three keys that can make an enormous difference.

The first is to act with constant and universal forgiveness and gentleness, without exception. To do that, we must be compassionate toward everything, including our self and our thoughts. We begin by making this a practice—a conscious practice. As we build on that practice, sooner or later it becomes our way of being in the world.

The second key has to do with surrendering our personal will to the Higher Will at every moment. That means not trying to control others or get our own way, but letting our heart guide us. In other words, try always to have your motives grounded in love. When you can do that, love and compassion toward others becomes your natural response.

Third, try not to take what others do personally, even when their actions seem to be directed toward you. This gets easier when we can remember that the other person is just trying to work through his or her own inner issues. As always, we have a choice. Instead of engaging with their negative energy, just keep sending them love.

While this may not be the whole answer, it certainly is a good place to begin.

Week 15. Taking a New Approach

Taking responsibility for my experiences was a totally new concept for me some 45 years ago. It had never occurred to me that my experiences were the result—to a very large extent—of the thoughts and feelings I was entertaining.

This taught me that how we see things, as well as the intentions we hold, can always be changed. There really is another way to view life and all of its circumstances.

Compassion is an important key to this process—compassion for yourself, for the mistakes you've made, the attitudes you've held. This is why learning to love and accept yourself—just the way you are—has been one of life's big lessons for me. Perhaps it is for you, too.

Yes, it can take a lot of work to make these inner changes, but you never have to do it alone. There is a Love that supports all of your efforts. When that Love is at work in you, you are blessed indeed.

Week 16. The Mind

I don't know if you've ever thought about it in this way, but your mind and your body are not the real "you." They are the instruments you are using while you are here on this planet.

Quite often, we just let our mind run rampant like a runaway car, making life more difficult than it already is, but it doesn't have to be that way. Your mind is a lot like the engine of your car. You steer your car where you want it to go. Similarly, you can steer your mind in the direction you want it to go. You can turn your mind away from negative, energy-draining emotions so you can think more clearly. In other words, you can choose how you want to respond to whatever comes along.

When you do this, you think what you really want to think so you can feel however you want to feel. The mind and the emotions are connected. When you guide one, you guide the other one, too. Always, you are the choice maker.

As we work with these principles, our perspective changes because we have changed our thinking. We hold healthier thoughts. Yes, and we begin to get glimpses of that "Great Expanse" the sages often spoke of.

The view from there is always worth the climb.

Week 17. We Lack Nothing

Do you have a special place where you like to go, a special hideaway perhaps, one that helps restore peace and calm in your life?

For me, that would be the ocean. Being there feeds me. It creates a sense of connection within me and leaves me feeling more whole.

But what if you can't get to your favorite place? What then?

I'm smiling, because you probably already know what I'm going to say.

When you can't get to your favorite place "out there," how about going to that special place inside you that opens during deep meditation? No thinking there, so no worries. You're just going home.

Eknath Easwaran calls this "the great gathering within" where all of our concerns, all of our anxieties and fears somehow are transformed into an inner peace which heals and restores us.

Every time we do this, we come back changed. If we continue this practice, little by little the realization dawns that deep down, we lack nothing. There is no limit to the wisdom, the love, the joy that can pour through us when we tune in to it. Our answers have always been within us!

Isn't this really what life is about? About finding the love? Finding the peace? Being the joy that is our natural state?

When that day comes, we begin to understand—truly understand—the meaning of gratitude.

Week 18. The Governing Factor

What is steering your ship of life? What is the governing factor around which everything else is weighed? In other words, what is the principle that is guiding you?

No doubt that could be different for all of us. Whatever that might be, there is one unalterable factor against which all of those choices are weighed. That factor is Love. The more we allow Love to steer our ship, the more open we are to the Higher Will.

Love moves us away from our self-ish interests and opens us to a broader spectrum where we aren't thinking just about ourself. Instead, we are thinking globally, where the best interests of all are considered.

If you are struggling with this concept, consider this: What you do to others, you do to yourself.

Yes, we are all connected. More than we know.

Week 19. Deepening Prayer

Many times our prayers are just a recital of our wants and concerns. If we truly want to have a conversation—better yet, a relationship—with God, then we need to be still and listen. When we do, we begin to sense His Presence. We hear His Voice. But how does that depth of listening come?

Through practice. By learning to let go of what we think we want so we can find out what God wants for us. This implies trust in the Wisdom that is seeking to guide us. I say that because even while we are seeking God, God is seeking us. Always, all He asks is our attention, our love, our trust.

When that becomes our posture, both when we are praying and when we aren't, we are aligning ourselves with His Higher Purpose for our life.

In return we receive both the comfort and the assurance of God's guiding hand.

Week 20. Parallel Callings

From time to time, selfless leaders appear on the world stage whose influence leaves an indelible mark on the lives of others. When I was growing up, Gandhi was one of those leaders, but there was another whose path closely aligned with Gandhi's. While we may not have been aware of Abdul Ghaffer Khan's alliance with Gandhi, how those two men lived their lives changed the culture of the people whom they served. Their example illustrated the lengths one must often go to put the needs of others above one's own. They showed their people what true dedication can accomplish when one is faithful to the call.

While it is true that most of us have not been called to follow either Gandhi's or Khan's path, it is also true that how we live our lives influences those around us far beyond the range of our own understanding.

Let us use the example of these two men to inspire us to live by our highest lights. For many of us, it is the most we have to offer.

Week 21. Managing Stress

Believe it or not, it really is possible to learn not to hurry, to not feel rushed, to not stress out over every little thing.

Stress is a toxin. It is also an emotion. If you don't learn how to manage those two elements, eventually your body will tell you about it.

Lowering the stress in your life is totally an inside job. Begin by paying attention to how you are moving through your day. When you find yourself rushing or feeling hurried, deliberately gear down. Take some slow deep breaths. In fact, make it a practice to just stop and b-r-e-a-t-h-e throughout your day.

While you are at it, try making room for a leisurely walk, a cup of tea, or whatever else may strike your fancy to help you gear down.

Find the time—every day—to be still. Even a few minutes here and there can make a difference. Better yet, start your day with some quiet time. Let it become part of the rhythm of your life.

As simple as these things may sound, they are proven survival techniques.

While you are at it, ask yourself what makes your heart sing? I mean, really sing? Whatever that is, reducing stress helps make that possible.

Week 22. Emotional Turbulence

Anger and its associated feelings are toxins. They eat away at our vitality and undermine our immune system. More than that, feeling angry leaves us with two problems—the original situation plus the negative emotions that affect our wellbeing at every level.

What we may not realize is that every time a storm rages within us, it sits there like a slow burning fire, creating space for more anger, more animosity, and moving us farther and farther away from the person we truly want to be.

That old law is true. Everything we do and everything we think has consequences. What to do? You can begin by learning to be aware of the thoughts and feelings that move you away from peace and love. Instead of entertaining every thought that comes into your head, simply cancel unwanted thoughts. It's a lot like turning off the TV. You just don't engage with them. In their place you affirm what really brings peace to your heart.

Anger divides us. It creates a mental and emotional sense of separation. It must then follow that when you are divided against others, you are also divided within yourself. If that is your experience, Eknath Easwaran suggests blessing whoever or whatever it was that upset you. The more you bless others, the less disturbed you will be by what they do or say.

What you are doing, of course, is learning to transform anger and all of its companions into love. While love may not be the whole answer, it certainly is a good place to begin.

Week 23. Anxiety

Sometimes it's just plain hard not to feel anxious about all of the uncertainty that surrounds us. When those times come, it is particularly important—and helpful—to remember that those anxious thoughts don't always originate with you. Much of what comes into your mind has its source in the collective consciousness. It just spins off from what others are thinking and feeling. The key is in knowing that you always have a choice in the thoughts that you allow yourself to entertain.

One of the problems with giving in to anxiety is that it moves us away from our spiritual center where peace resides. We can have peace or we can have anxiety, but we can't have both. So let's all start being aware of the thoughts we're hearing inside us and then choose what we really want to fill our mind.

I'm not talking about hiding our collective heads in the sand. What I am saying is if we really want peace, we have to pay more attention to the thoughts we are entertaining, because those thoughts are filling our days. How we spend our days is how we spend our life.

Week 24. Finding the "Up" Side

During this most unusual time, when just plain ordinary routines are being disrupted by unfamiliar restrictions, one's life can seem out of kilter. The balance we have been accustomed to feels disturbed, but whenever there is a "down side," there is always an "up" side, too.

Perhaps these restrictions are giving us an opportunity to come away from all of the busy-ness we have become accustomed to so we can focus more on who we really are. What is our purpose in life? Why are we here? Just what is it that will satisfy the deep longing in our soul?

What I am talking about has to do with making the effort to consciously connect with our Creator. How we do that will be different for each of us, but do it we must if we are ever to find the peace we are seeking.

What better time than now?

Week 25. Keeping Afloat

Challenge is part of life, but no matter how difficult something may seem, there is always a way. Your trials, your conflicts and your challenges can actually empower you. They can awaken something within you that has been waiting to bloom when you can trust the Love that is guiding you. That Love supports you, whether you see it or not. Yes, and that Love is sustaining you, even in your darkest moments.

No matter how difficult life may seem, you do have it within you to press on. While it is true that grief, despair, and feeling discouraged are all natural responses, remaining there is always a choice.

Absolutely anything is possible once you learn to own your choices. Learning to do that is one of life's big lessons. It's one of the ways we learn to keep afloat.

Week 26. About Elections

Elections certainly do gives us an opportunity to practice accepting what is, even when "what is" may be contrary to our strongly-held hopes and beliefs.

There is much in life that we cannot change. Election results would certainly be one of them. Once the votes have all been counted, the practice for all of us would be to accept what is, even if the outcome is very different from what we had hoped for.

That will be asking a lot for many of us. If you are like me, sometimes I really, really, really want the outcome of an election to go a certain way. Maybe you do, too, but we aren't in control, and never will be. What is the next best thing?

Well, we could trust that God is leading us in the direction that will allow us to learn what we need to learn so we can be what we are meant to be.

Dr. David Hawkins says we can afford to surrender to what is. Why? Because God is in all things.

Week 27. Jesus' Example

We can learn a lot from how Jesus showed his love to the people he interacted with. Never did he look down on others. Instead, he sought to lift them up and leave them feeling better about themselves, regardless of who they were or what they had done. He encouraged them. Even those who sought to destroy him were met with compassion and patience. He gave others every possible opportunity to reach for the highest within themselves. His was an ennobling spirit, one that was gracious and kind, regardless of how he was treated.

If we can take just one quality from that list and make it our own, we will have accomplished a lot. What we're talking about is learning to love others as God loves us. That means everyone. No exceptions.

Without a love like that, how can hope and peace ever come alive in our hearts?

Week 28. Just Breathe!

Wherever I look, I see people running, running, running, trying to get everything done. It makes me wonder if we've forgotten about our responsibility to ourself. The body can't go at that pace forever. What to do?

Well, instead of running, running, running, how about breathing, breathing, breathing instead?

When I say, "breathe," I mean breathe deeply. Breathe slowly.

This is important. Every cell in your body is dependent on oxygen! Unfortunately, when we are tired or are feeling stressed, we tend to take shallow breaths, but that isn't good enough. Why? Because the body gets the oxygen it needs from the bottom of the lungs, not the top.

Slow deep breathing—conscious breathing—gives your body the oxygen it needs, thereby strengthening the lungs and increasing your stamina.

The mind and the breath work in tandem. The more agitated we are, the more rapid and shallow our breathing becomes. Try paying attention to your breath whenever you can. Watching your breath keeps your attention in the present moment and really does release stress.

Remember, feeling stressed is a choice, so try doing just one thing at a time instead of multi-tasking. Then you can actually enjoy what you are doing without depleting your energy and overloading your system.

Whenever you feel you don't have enough time, stop and breathe. Slowly and deeply. Your body will thank you.

Week 29. Something to Consider

We are all looking out of different "windows" that have been created by countless factors. Consequently, no two of us are going to see things in exactly the same way. Yet having different points of view does not make one of us wrong, even though it may seem so.

Only God knows what the real truth is. In the meantime, let's try listening to each other with kindness, humility, and consideration.

What we do have in common—and will always have in common—is that we are all God's children, and we are all growing in understanding. The fact that we aren't "there" yet would certainly be cause for compassion, especially when our views differ greatly.

Here is an unknown poet's answer to how can we see each other more clearly:

"How could I not love you? You are what I am. How could I hate you? I am what you are."

Week 30. Blooming

Wendell Berry believes that even the darkness blooms and sings. I agree. One morning when I woke up, I saw a new bloom opening on my 50+-year-old Chinese Evergreen. Was it the work of the night? Perhaps, but how many nights did it take before that one bud appeared?

There, in the comfort of the dark soil, a force—a desire to bloom—was at work. But what about before that? It took over 50 years for that bloom to appear!

One can only think that silent, unseen forces were at work—are always at work—while we just go about our days completely oblivious to the great creative energy that surrounds us, seeking to bloom through us, too.

Have you ever thought about this? Just what does this creative energy want to do through you? Are you willing to follow its lead?

No one else can follow that call in just the way you can. That just may be why life keeps knocking on your door.

Week 31. Finding Order in the Chaos

It is only natural to want to be in control, but we are never in control. Not completely. Trying to control everything in your life is like trying to control the wind. It consumes a lot of energy and depletes your system.

Whether we know it or not, even whether it seems like it or not, this moment is as it should be. There is order in the chaos. There is purpose behind the upheaval. I say that because there really is an infinite organizing power that is continually working to create beauty out of dissolution and peace out of discord.

In the meantime, what can you do? Well, when life gets hectic, see if you can let go of how you want your life to be so you can accept how it is. That is one of our greatest lessons. Those lessons contain the potential for some of our greatest blessings.

Wisdom tells us to make peace with the fact that it just isn't going to be possible to have it all or do it all during this one lifetime. Slow down and enjoy the gifts each moment brings, for truly, you lack nothing.

You see, the pieces really do all fit together. They always have. We just can't see the whole picture. It's our point of view that causes our confusion.

I find it comforting to know that there is a rhythm and a reason for all of this. When that view does finally open up to us, we will be the wiser for it.

Week 32. Turbulence

When change comes into your life—especially great change, you can be sure you are being given a chance to grow. But what if that change turned your life upside down? What if it feels as though you got stuck on a roller coaster and all you can do is hang on?

Dr. David Morehouse says sometimes turbulence is necessary to move us into the next chapter of our life where growth is imminent,

21

so don't be afraid of what life brings. When those times come, there is one thing of which you can be certain—there is something you are ready to learn. Whatever it is, it's probably important, so let life teach you. Let it lead you. Let it help you find the path that is waiting for you at this particular time in your life.

With all my heart, I promise you won't regret it.

Week 33. Choosing

Author Byron Katie tells us problems are only possible when we believe what we're thinking. If she is right, and I believe she is, then the good news is you don't have to believe every thought that comes into your head! If a thought comes along that you aren't sure about, or that you don't like, ask yourself how you would feel if the thought wasn't true. Is this something you want to believe or not? You can always choose thoughts more to your liking.

A different thought, a different way of seeing something, can change the context of a situation entirely. What we once thought was a problem can turn into a great blessing.

It's all in how we view it, in what we choose to believe.

Week 34. You Are Secure, Regardless

Life is like a river—it is constantly changing. Sometimes those changes make life seem chaotic, but that description just reflects our point of view. According to Deepak, chaos simply means the universe is re-arranging itself.

Actually, chaos is a natural part of the creative process. I'll never forget hearing Deepak tell us it takes chaos to create a dancing star. I'd not thought of it in quite those terms, but it does make sense. Sometimes it takes chaos (aka re-arranging) to create something new. While that can be unsettling, there is order—even a purpose—within the chaos.

How does that principle apply to us? Certainly we would want to make every effort to meet the demands of our situation. While we are doing that, it helps a lot if we can remember that life is bringing something into our life that has the potential to strengthen our trust and faith. You see, there actually is order within the chaos. Whatever is going on, we are being held securely within an eternal, unchanging, underlying framework.

Regardless of what is happening, in the silence of our soul, everything is always all right. When we are anchored in that sacred inner space, we can ride the waves, knowing that the Powers That Be are always working toward our highest good.

Week 35. Your Inner Axle

Sri Nisargadatta Marahaj advises us to always be anchored in our deep center, no matter where we go or what we are doing. That deep center is our balance point. It is where all begins.

Just as our planet turns on its own balance point, so must we be anchored in our own deep center instead of whirling around the periphery.

Why is this so important? The nature of that axle is Love.

Week 36. The Call

No doubt you've had moments—as have I—when the beauty of Nature and the magnificence of Creation literally stops you in your tracks and causes you to reflect on something so vast, so deep, that words cannot describe it. It can be something as beautiful as a sunset or as grand as a mountain range. That which has touched you reminds you—perhaps even reflects back to you—what author John O'Donohue calls your own inner magnificence. You sense a connection so deep that words cannot describe it. That connection is your link to the vast terrain deep within you which is ever calling to you.

To hear that call and answer is to turn toward your eternal home.

Week 37. The Deeper We Go

If there is one thing I have learned, it is that the deeper we go, the greater the gift. Once we become aware of what that gift actually is, we also become aware of the boundless Mercy and eternal Love that has been steering us through whatever we were facing.

Always that immeasurable Presence is here, just waiting for us to awaken to how it is forever at work in our life.

Week 38. Your Message

No doubt we've all had people in our lives whose presence acted as a guiding light to us. Their example never leaves us.

My father was one of those people for me. He was the absolute essence of integrity. Although he never talked about it, integrity was the standard by which he lived his life. Whenever I'm struggling with a decision, I think about Daddy and try to discern what choice he would make.

Another person who touched me deeply was Gandhi. When I was growing up, Gandhi was a moving force on the planet. Back then, there was no TV. We would hear about what he was doing to free the Indian people from British domination by way of the newspaper or the radio. Better still, we actually got to see Gandhi in the newsreels at the movie theater. This was back in those early days of news communication when "movie films" were just coming in. The only way you could actually see what was happening in the world was to go to the theater and watch the news which was always shown between the featured films.

That is how I got to hear Gandhi speak. I watched him lead thousands of people to the sea where they gathered salt to protest the British dictum that required them to buy their salt only from the British government (at outrageous prices). I saw Gandhi walk from village to village with Abdul Ghaffer Khan, his compatriot from the Northwest Territory who was on a similar mission for his people. I listened with a deep ear to what they were teaching their people about the principle of nonviolence, how it is rooted and grounded in love and service. All of this left such a deep impression on me that I can still hear—still see—them in my mind's eye.

It wasn't until years later, when I was reading Eknath Easwaran's book, *Gandhi the Man*, that I came across a passage telling how a reporter stopped Gandhi one time as he was boarding a train. The reporter asked for a message he could take back to his readers. Gandhi quickly replied, "My life is my message!"

It was true for Gandhi, it was true for my father, and it is true for you and me.

Week 39. Deep Inner Work

Dr. David Hawkins reminds us that while it is easy to blame our problems on someone or something else, actually the root of the discord we experience in life has to do with how we respond to what is happening. That means we must become aware of the choices we are making. We must acknowledge the thoughts and feelings that pull us down. Then we let go of that negative energy over and over, until every last bit of it is gone.

Hawkins says this is a lot like cleaning a dirty window. The cleaner our "window" gets, the easier it is to find the unconditional love that is at the very core of our being.

It takes courage and honesty to embrace this deep healing work. The beautiful thing about it is that when we allow this healing power to open us up to our truest self, everyone benefits.

As Dr. Hawkins once said, when the ocean rises, so do all the ships upon it. In the same way, when love is able to flow through the human heart, all beings are blessed by it.

Week 40. Three More Keys

Just as a ship's navigator needs a compass, so do we need an inner spiritual compass to steer us through life's challenges. To that end, I would like to offer three more keys that Dr. Hawkins recommends:

1. Faith – As I see it, if God can create this vast universe and all of the wonders in it, including you and me, He can certainly guide us through whatever difficulties we may encounter.

2. Devotion – When we go through turbulent times, we would do well to ask ourselves just exactly what we are devoted to. My dictionary defines devotion as "allegiance, commitment, dedication." While there are other meanings for this word, these particular definitions shed light on how to keep our faith strong. Regardless of what may be happening in our lives, if we truly have faith in the Lord, then we will trust in His guidance, instead of allowing fear to take over.

3. Surrender – That's a big one, isn't it, but what exactly are we being asked to surrender? Perhaps to the illusion that how we see things is always right. Can we admit to ourselves that our perspective is limited, that there is a wider, grander view which can open to us when we are willing to look beyond what we think we know? Why cling to a limited view when there is so much more just waiting to illumine our understanding?

What all this really means is to let go of the controls and let God steer your ship. As I see it, there isn't a better Navigator around.

Week 41. Finding Balance

Balance is key to a happy, healthy life, but what about those times when everything seems out of balance? Our life, our families, our work, even our planet? According to Eckhart Tolle, the answer is stillness, but how can we find it?

Well, we could begin by quieting our noisy, anxious mind and all of its busy thinking. We could open our heart and let all of that inner turmoil out. We could drain the pump dry until all that is left is the peace of simply being.

When all of that inner discord is gone, what is left to worry about? What is there to fear? When we are anchored in peace and trust, we truly know that God is still in control, that a Higher Wisdom is guiding us all. As Tolle reminds us, we can lose ourselves in the world, or we can lose ourselves (and all of our concerns) in peace. Perhaps—just perhaps—this "global crisis" is Nature's way of giving us a chance to re-set our anchor.

Up until now, we've been like children wandering through the woods, continually lost in thought, yet there is a part of us that still hears the universe singing its eternal song. This is the part of us that is always aware, the part that sees and knows with inner eyes.

Let's all learn to see through those eyes and hear through those ears.

Week 42. Like A River

"Nothing can disturb the calm peace of my soul" is one of the primary truths the ancient sages gave us. When I first heard that statement many years ago, I was astonished. I didn't see how that could be possible, but they were right.

What was true for them is true for us, too. The peace they spoke of is always here, always within us. All we have to do is go within where we can connect with the peace that is the very ground of our being.

Recently I had the opportunity to watch a beautiful river. Sometimes the river was so still, it was like a mirror. Other times, when the water was more active, the light danced on the water. Just being able to be there and watch it was such a gift.

One day, when the surface of the river was like glass, a little boat came drifting along. As it moved silently through the water, ripples slowly began spreading out from the front of the boat. Gradually, yet oh so quietly, they spread until they reached from shore to shore.

As I watched that beautiful scene, I couldn't help thinking how we are a lot like that. I say that because when you are at peace, we all are touched by it.

Week 43. Just Love Each Other

We all know how important it is to forgive each other, but has it ever occurred to you that if we hadn't thought something was "bad," the need to forgive wouldn't even be there? What if we could acknowledge that whatever others did or are doing is the best they have to offer at that particular moment? What if that was true of us as well?

What if we could accept each other, just the way we are, without judging? Wouldn't that take us beyond the need to forgive? What if we could just love each other in spite of our differences, in spite of what may or may not sit quite right with us?

The wonder of it—at least in my eyes—is that when we can choose to love each other unconditionally, not only does it free others from the burden of our judgment, it frees us, too.

Week 44. A Promise

Just as the sun shines down upon us all, so does God's Love surround and enfold us. Wherever we are, whatever we may be doing, in the midst of all of our experiences, God's Love is here with us, supporting us, showing us the way.

In God's Love, there is no fear, nor is there any judgment. There is only Love—pure, unconditional Love and Acceptance—just the way we are.

We are all growing. We are all evolving into greater levels of understanding. That is the nature of the process we are moving through. All of these life experiences—yes, all of them—contribute to that growth and understanding.

No doubt you've heard all of this before, but on this particular morning it seems important to say once again that God's Infinite Loving Presence is always with you, always supporting you.

No matter what is happening in your life, just remember—that Presence and that Support is always there. You never have to walk through life alone.

Week 45. Seeking Answers

Sometimes answers come to me in ways I never could have thought of, let alone orchestrated, all because I kept asking my questions over and over. While I was waiting for answers, I admit I would think about how I might solve the problem, but always there seemed to be a hand in front of my face and an inner voice that kept saying, "Not yet. Just wait. Be patient," so I waited. The waiting wasn't easy, but when the answers did come, it was pretty obvious that only a Divine Hand could have orchestrated them.

I tell you this because whatever is in the process of being developed in the unseen field of the cosmos will come when all of the pieces are in place, and not before. In the meantime, your part is to trust, be patient, and keep asking your questions.

God is always at work on your behalf. When your answers do come, you will understand why waiting was necessary.

Week 46. Inner Growth

Oftentimes inner growth can feel like a solitary journey. It takes great courage to hold your course on the seas of life when it seems like no one is there to cheer you on. Not to despair.

When you do press on, when you don't give up, the wind of the Spirit catches your sail and carries you along. It is then you realize you were never really alone.

Week 47. Difficult Changes

Sudden change, especially great change, can leave us facing what some would call the Great Unknown, leaving us in totally unfamiliar territory with no idea of how to move forward. We can feel lost, confused, with no idea of where to go or what to do next.

While times such as these are part of life, That which has brought you to this moment will also carry you through it. I say this because no matter how great the upheaval, all is not lost, only changed.

When those times come, just know there is a way. There is always a way. It is waiting for you even now, so trust in the process. Trust in the Hand which is always here to guide you.

No matter how dark the night, morning always comes.

Week 48. Thoughts Manifest!

Deepak says the character of our predominant thought stream shows us what our future will be like. As long as our thoughts are healthy, the future will flow into the present moment naturally.

Thoughts begin as a sort of blueprint. When we believe those thoughts, they take on substance. They shape our ideas and beliefs, which in turn color our point of view.

It was a good reminder. Our thoughts do create our days, whether we know it or not.

Week 49. A More Stable Position

Life is full of lessons, at least that is how it has been for me. One of the things I have learned along the way is that the only thing we can control is how we respond to what is going on around us. That understanding makes all the difference. Yes, challenges will still come, but this new perspective makes it possible for us to meet them from a more stable position.

The next time something difficult comes along, try seeing it as an exercise—even an opportunity—to practice being a conscious choice maker. This much I can promise—whatever you choose will determine the nature of the outcome.

Week 50. Life Lessons

Our trials and tribulations are so rich with promise. It may not seem like it at the time, but they are. Nothing is ever wasted. The potential for growth—and new life—is hidden in even the most difficult of situations. All things do indeed come bearing a gift if we can just hang in there long enough to find it.

It helps if we can accept and embrace what is. That means being open enough to let go of judgment—of yourself, and others, and even the challenge itself. Letting go of our expectations opens us to a higher plan. Surrender fits well here. Not my will, but Thine.

Eventually you find out that your life isn't just about you. It's about all of us. That means wanting for others the same things we yearn for so deeply. May we all be blessed.

It's been quite a journey. The more I've learned, the more convinced I am that life isn't about "things." It's about being your highest and best.

Week 51. Listening

When we tune in to our deep inner wisdom and listen for guidance, we are actually communing with our Source. That communion is what meditation is all about—connecting with our Source where we can experience our deeper connection.

Thousands of years ago the ancient yogis discovered that the deeper they listened, the more they experienced the truth of Who They Really Were. The same can happen for us—and will—when we learn to tune in to a deeper level of our being.

Experiential knowledge changes everything, including how you see yourself and how you live your life. A subtle rhythm seems to take over as you move in sync with what the Lord has in mind for you. Then you know—absolutely know—that "you" aren't really "doing" anything. It's all being done through you.

Week 52. The Mystery

When we criticize or judge, we create a world of criticism and judgment for ourselves. The law is inescapable—we receive exactly what we give. To move beyond whatever is disturbing us, we must let be what is. This means no resistance in the heart, only full acceptance of what is, whether we like "what is" or not.

We do this by letting go fully and completely of whatever perceived wrong we are clinging to, even when our heart may be saying, "even this for this?" The answer is an unqualified "Yes." It is only when we let go of the perceived hurt/wrong/problem that we will be free to move on with our life.

Always these burdens are carried within us, and that is where the work must be done. The more openhearted we are, the more we experience God's grace in our lives.

All things do come to bless us. That is the mystery which we work to unravel every day of our lives.

Year Two

Week 53. When It Is the Darkest

As we turn our thoughts toward new beginnings, I am particularly mindful of the many ways in which Nature offers her silent messages of peace, new life, and hope. Nature is continually reminding us of our eternal newness. Even this very moment has never happened before. We are always at a new beginning.

The new moon in January is an eloquent reminder of this. We will also have just passed the turn of the New Year. Before that was the winter solstice. That solstice marked the beginning of the deepest time of winter.

As you probably already know, the winter solstice marks both the "shortest" day and the "longest" night. What is not commonly known is that during that longest time of darkness, the earth is—and we are—actually closest to the sun.

What a wonderful analogy that is, and what a powerful reminder that during our greatest times of darkness, we are closest to the light.

I find great comfort in that thought. I hope you do, too.

Week 54. Trusting the Divine Plan

Dr. David Hawkins promises that those who continue on their upward climb do make a difference in the global consciousness. While it is also true that our efforts do not fully resolve the world's problems, he also says we should not be discouraged. If we truly trust in the overall design of our Creator, then we can safely surrender the fate of our world to our God. We can do this because all that is happening, on whatever scale, is always in sync with the Higher Wisdom that is governing our world.

As we humbly surrender whatever is happening to that Wisdom, let us not forget that we best serve that Divine Plan through how we live our lives.

Week 55. When the Load Gets Heavy

It is so important to take care of yourself when the load gets heavy. I found that out the hard way. That's why I've said over and over that you absolutely must nurture yourself if you want to be able to give out of your fullness instead of your dregs.

Easy to say, but hard to do? Here are some suggestions to help you lighten up and take the pressure off:

1. What is it you really need right now? Then find a way to do it! No excuses!

2. What brings a smile to your face? Then do it!

3. Stop and have a cup of tea. Better yet, have that tea with a friend or family member. Warm tea can be comforting, the company of someone else even more so.

4. Is there a book you've been wanting to read? Give yourself permission to curl up with it and forget the world for a while.

5. Bring flowers or a blooming plant into your home to honor your loved ones. Flowers mean life, and there is always life, both here and in the hereafter. Flowers are a beautiful way to honor the life you've shared with others.

6. Laugh every chance you can find. If you have to, fake it until you make it. Laughter is healing. Hearty laughter gets the endorphins going and lifts the spirit. Read funny books, watch a funny movie. Laughter picks you up and leaves you in a lighter place.

7. Get out and walk! Every day, if you can. If the weather won't allow you to walk outside, then do it inside, either in your home

or in a mall. I have a treadmill in my home, but when I'm not in the mood for the treadmill, then I "do the loop" around my house for twenty minutes. Did you know you can laugh while you're walking? Try it! Just trying it makes you feel like laughing.

8. If you have favorite recipes or just plain comfort foods you particularly enjoy, this would be an excellent time to enjoy them. Give yourself permission to fix them. It's just another way to nurture both body and soul.

9. Listen to what your body is asking for. If it wants rest, then rest. If it really doesn't want to do something, then don't do it. Your body knows what is best for you at any given moment. Whenever you are in doubt about something, listen to your body. Your body never lies.

10. Find a way to reach out and help others. Ask your heart how you can help, how you can serve. Compassionate living takes our attention off ourselves and eases our burdens.

11. Fill your days—and your heart—with gratitude. You might begin by making a list of all of the many ways you've been blessed. If you're like me, the list never ends.

12. Lastly, but certainly not least, Brother Lawrence suggests taking mini-retreats with God throughout the day. Even if only for a moment or two, that conscious inner connection rights our ship and brings us back in balance. The more we do this, the easier it becomes to maintain a relationship with—and an awareness of—God's presence no matter where we are or what we are doing. This means that we walk with God, we talk with Him, we rest in Him, and we listen for His guidance. If Brother Lawrence could learn to do that, surely we can, too!

Week 56. The Journey

I'll never forget the first time I heard Deepak talk about being a conscious choice maker. His words really rang my bell. That's when I knew deep inside myself that regardless of what was going on, how it affected my life was up to me.

This is such an important key, particularly when we've broken loose from our moorings and don't yet know where we are going. Andre' Gide tells us we cannot discover new lands without consenting to lose sight of the shore for a very long time. He is right.

The good news is that there is always a power greater than we are that knows where we are going and how we are to get there. When we trust in that Wisdom, then each day—and each step of the way—becomes more precious as life unfolds before us.

Week 57. An Answer

Whenever we offer a loving response, a gentle gesture, or even something as simple as a hug, we are actually tapping into the depths of what relationships are all about. Yes, I know. That isn't always easy to do. Especially if something turned your world upside down and you just don't know what to do.

Those are the times when love is the most powerful—and the most needed. That is why we meditate. That is why we settle into the quiet depths within us where nothing is wrong, where there is only love and, to quote Eknath Easwaran, resentment is impossible.

This is a skill. As with any skill, it takes practice to really make it our own. What better investment could we make in ourself and our relationships than to find that sacred place within us where we are all one and there is only love?

We are all doing the best we can at any given time. Anchoring our daily life in those loving depths within us quiets those stormy seas and opens us to the indescribable peace that only the soul knows.

When we are anchored in that sacred inner place, we know that no matter what the problem might be, the answer—at least in part—is love.

Week 58. Living in Sync

Our intentions play a big part in the way our lives unfold. Holding steadfast to an intention sets things in motion that make it possible for the intention to manifest, but there is an overriding factor. The Higher Will is always geared toward bringing us whatever is best for us in the long run. It might bring something better than what we asked for, or something different, or even a challenge of some kind that will cause us to grow so we can be ready for that next higher step.

The more we are aligned with the Higher Will, the more we are able to live and move in sync with what is highest and best for us. Meditation is one of the best ways there is to bring ourself into alignment. The more we reach into that inner domain, the more our own personal frequency becomes attuned to and aligned with that Higher Will. Then we just automatically move beyond the things that would have disturbed us.

Alignment is one of the major benefits meditation offers.

Week 59. Living at Our Deepest Levels

Sometimes, when we move into the stillness of meditation, we lose all sense of boundaries and find ourself in a state of simply being. Not thinking. Not doing. Just being. That boundless sense of awareness opens us to a deeper level of identity where we know we are so much more than the thoughts or feelings that usually fill our waking hours. It is as though a window has opened and we are given a glimpse of who we truly are.

As we continue with our practice, a spiritual energy enfolds us and we begin seeing life more from an inner stance. This new perspective colors all we do and say. As we settle into this new way of being, we begin moving in harmony with That which ever seeks to guide us.

Yes, there will still be challenges. That is how we grow, but now we see these difficult times more as an opportunity to continue on our upward climb. When we can accept—rather than struggle against—those challenging moments, we allow a Greater Reality to show us the direction we are meant to go.

When we do this, we are truly learning to live at our deepest levels.

Week 60. As a Seed

As you progress in your spiritual studies, you will probably come across something you don't understand. It could be a new way of saying something, or it could be something you've just not thought about before. Whatever it is, rather than struggling with the concept, just let it be as a seed inside you. Let it rest and ripen there, without any effort from you. When the time is right, the blossom of new understanding will appear as though from out of nowhere, and you will smile over its unexpected appearance.

Real Truth is like that. It grows within us, just waiting for the time when our vision is wide enough to glimpse the broader horizon that is always waiting for us.

Yes, resting, waiting and trusting can be a very fruitful time.

Week 61. A Fresh Approach to Anger

Knowing that anger is a choice doesn't mean it will be easy to keep calm when something hits your trigger. This being true, here is a fresh approach that might be of some help: If you don't get angry, you don't have to calm down!

Just think of the difference that would make!

Week 62. All Is Well

Did you know that change and uncertainty are part of the overall order of things? It's true! What we don't always recognize is that there is an ongoing purpose to that fluidity. In fact, it's part of the plan! You see, there would be no growth without change. With no growth, there is no life. Yes, change definitely plays an important part in how things unfold.

Even in the midst of change, we are held securely by the Higher Power that is at work in us. That is why we can say that all is well and all shall be well, regardless. Even when we don't like what is happening, the deeper purpose is always for our highest good.

There is so much to learn. Much of that learning happens through circumstances we could never have orchestrated or even asked for. When things seem uncertain, just know that everything is working together to bring you the best possible result.

Who could ask for more than that?

Week 63. The Best Investment

Dr. David Morehouse suggests choosing one quality you'd like to strengthen and making that your overriding goal. It can be anything—compassion, love, patience, forgiveness—you name it.

What is that one thing you know you need to work on? Once you've figured that out, start there. Once that quality becomes your guiding principle—once it is established in you and your life—add another quality to your practice.

What he's talking about is building an inner foundation of spiritual values that will carry you through all of your days, no matter what.

If this speaks to you, then why not start now? It's the best investment you can make.

Week 64. An Easier Way

So often, when we encounter a difficulty, our immediate and natural response is to try to figure out what to do about it. The easier—and often forgotten—response would be to simply turn it over to the Lord and ask for guidance. "How do you want me to do this, Lord? What can I learn from this? Is there a deeper purpose at work here?" These questions align us with God's eternal purpose that is always at work in our life.

Whenever we begin with God, things just seem to take care of themselves. Yes, we still have our part to do, but that part is so much easier when we know that the Spirit of the Lord is going before us, making happy and successful our way.

Week 65. Together We Will Triumph

We are such a vast sea of humanity. I have often wondered what difference one person can make. If you are wondering about this, too, try putting a drop of ink into a bowl of water and see what happens. The ink spreads, doesn't it? All the water changes color. I know that's a rather simple way of describing what we are talking about, but it is a good analogy. When you are healed, we all share in your wholeness. When you suffer, we all suffer.

In one way or another, and to one extent or another, we do indeed share our common lot. Whether we know it or not, even whether we want to or not, every bit of progress you make is progress for us all. Every bit of courage you muster is just that much more courage for each one of us. All of the ways you find to triumph over the challenges of life elevate our collective spirit that much more. And as you discover and grow into your truest self, so do we all.

I am reminded of mountain climbers going up the side of a mountain, each one connected to the other through the life-line, the rope that ties them together. In a very real sense, one person's ascent is the next person's toe-hold. When one is safe, when one is secure, they all are. When one is in danger, they all are.

We are a lot like that, and therein lies a responsibility that cannot be denied. As we search for our highest and best, it is not just we alone who will benefit. Every bit of progress means just that much more progress for the whole of humanity.

While it is true that such lofty goals are rarely at the front of our thinking when we are struggling with great challenge, it can be fortifying to know that it is not for ourself alone that we struggle. It is not just for ourself that we search for light to guide us. We are all searching, even when we least know it. When I am at my weakest you may be at your strongest. When you are beset with difficulties, there will be others who are "feeding the pump." It matters not when or who, for we are in this together. We each must meet our own challenges, but it is together that we will triumph.

Week 66. Solitude

If you had a whole day of peace and quiet, how would it feel? What would you do? What would you think about? What would you be? Who would you be? Important questions, to be sure, and certainly worth thinking about. Where else are we going to find the answers we long for if it isn't within ourself? Oh yes, we look to others for our answers, but when we do, isn't it more for confirmation of what we already inwardly sense to be true?

If these are questions you've been asking yourself, perhaps it is time to stop and take stock of your situation. What would you like your life to be like now? Is there something you'd really like to do? Do you have hopes and dreams that have yet to be fulfilled? This may be the time to begin pursuing them.

What would make life more meaningful for you now? Is there a passion burning within you, some long-held desire to develop a skill or a talent? These answers are in your heart. They are part of the fabric of your being.

When you listen to what your heart is saying, you find new meaning and purpose for your days.

41

Week 67. Our Growing Times

Certainly times of change are stretching, learning, growing times. As we expand in awareness of our nature and our potential, we may feel excited yet somewhat uneasy with the promise of unlimited growth. How can we be ready to be more when we are not yet comfortable with what we are now? It is a question that has no answer, but perhaps it does not need one. The process is so subtle that it happens without our even knowing it. We might just as soon try to watch the grass grow, but grow it does, and so do we—in just the right way, and at just the right time.

The process is more a flow than a happening, with no beginning and no ending. Inner qualities and inner truth just surface like bubbles of reality in our consciousness as they emerge in our awareness unannounced and unexpected. It is a birthing process, a becoming so interior in its occurrence that only in the silence can it creep into our awareness. Indeed, were we not looking we would never know it was there, but it is there. It is the stuff of life that molds and shapes us, that brings a new dynamic into our experience and gives it both meaning and purpose as we encounter the truths we have been seeking.

In that birthing, subtle and sometimes unseen, is the undeniable need to let go. Only when we do can the miracle truly happen.

Week 68. A Healing Space

It isn't easy to make friends with the loneliness we sometimes feel after the loss of a loved one. Loneliness is certainly a natural response to our loss, and yet, if we are patient, if we are willing to work through it to its deeper side, the quiet that is now such a part of our life can become a healing space for us. If we pay attention to this sense of presence, it can grow into an expanded state of awareness where the silence of our soul is reflected back to us. When we rest in that silence, we become more attuned to our inner self. We begin to realize that silence is at the very core of our nature. Because it is our nature, that silence and that peace are always there waiting for us.

This silent place, then, becomes our haven, our place of deep repose. We can always go there. All it takes is a subtle shift of attention from "out there" to "in here" and we are home.

Thus our loneliness is transformed into solitude, into that inner place where we can renew and restore all that was thrown out of balance.

Week 69. On Resistance

When we are feeling challenged, it is easy to think of our situation as bad or difficult, yet it is neither. It simply is what it is. Resistance is what colors it with a negative hue.

Deepak says there is an hierarchy of needs for each one of us that we are born to fulfill. When we can look at things from this higher perspective, we can see that our challenges have a positive purpose in that they help us grow. When we have learned to accept and work with what is, then the higher good takes over and we begin seeing things from a new perspective.

Even in the most difficult of circumstances, try allowing things to be what they are instead of resisting them. Then you can grow how life wants you to grow with serenity and with peace.

Always the universe has your highest good in mind and is supporting you every step of the way.

Week 70. True Happiness

I used to look for happiness in the things around me. I would tell myself, "If only I had this…" or "If I could just do that…" Do you know what I discovered? That kind of happiness never lasts! Why do you suppose that is? Simply put, when we look to "things" for our happiness, we are looking in the wrong place!

True happiness—lasting happiness—goes hand in hand with the peace, joy and love we find when we are aligned with our Higher Self. When we are in tune with That, happiness just naturally follows.

43

Whenever feelings of discontent come to visit, just remind yourself that the solution is never "out there." We must always look within.

Week 71. Aurobindo

The great Indian sage, Aurobindo, tells us that our grief and our stumbling are the result of not knowing who we are. He assures us that when we tune in to the pure inner essence that truly defines us, we will be able to move through any crisis and remain untouched. Changed, yes, but untouched, all because the nature of our own indwelling Truth is Peace.

Week 72. It Isn't About You

Oftentimes, when people lash out verbally or otherwise, they are reacting to something that is beyond their control. Even though they think the problem is "out there," actually there is an inner issue that can only be resolved by inner work.

If you just happen to be "handy" when people need to vent, instead of taking it personally, try to remember that what they are really doing is asking for help. Venting may be the only way they know how to do that.

Looking beyond someone's anger to the frustration and powerlessness they are feeling makes it easier for you to respond in a compassionate manner. You can do that when you understand that whatever the issue is, it isn't about you. It's about love.

Whenever you bring love into someone's life, you both are blessed.

Week 73. Our Thoughts

I'm guessing you probably don't let everyone who shows up at your door come into your home. In the same way, we should be just as vigilant regarding our thoughts.

Thoughts are magnetic energy patterns. This means the more we think a particular thought, the more it attracts similar thoughts to us. Before long we've created a habitual thought pattern. Then we wonder why certain things keep happening in our life.

The answer is simple. (Not easy, but simple!) Change your thoughts and you change your experience! Just start where you are and bring your thinking more in line with what you really want your life to be like.

While you can't control or change everything that comes into your life, you can always change your thoughts. Begin there.

Week 74. Laugh!

Laughter is the best tonic around, so laugh every chance you get! Believe it or not, 10 minutes of hearty laughter is equal to 30 minutes of any aerobic activity! What could be easier than that?

Laughter provides deep relief—mentally, emotionally and physically. A good session of laughter reduces stress and lifts your spirit, making it easier for your body to restore and renew itself. Laughter strengthens the immune system and improves blood circulation. It even helps reduce age-related illnesses!

Laughter therapists say we should start and end our days with laughter. They even suggest laughing for 5 minutes before we get out of bed in the morning, and again when we are ready to end our day!

Laughter is an excellent way to jump-start your system when you need a lift. But don't just believe me. Try it for yourself and see the difference it makes!

Week 75. Why Meditate?

Prayer is when we talk to God. Meditation is when we listen. Yes, a good diet, appropriate exercise, adequate rest are all important, but meditating is the single most important thing you can do to restore balance and harmony in your body and in your life, so meditate every day. If you don't yet know how, find someone who can teach you.

Meditation can be your anchor, your safe haven, your balance point. When we meditate, we rest in the eternality of our spirit where there is no time, where all things happen exactly as they are supposed to.

Meditating connects you to the part of yourself that is always at peace, that is never afraid, never sick. I am talking about your soul. When you are anchored in that sacred center, a new perspective opens to you, one that allows you to see beyond any challenge to the growth—and the blessings—that must inevitably follow.

Week 76. Our Deeper Song

While we may be able to track the farthest star, even listen to its song, what seems to have escaped the range of our listening is our hearts. There is a song that has always been singing within us. To hear it we have to pay attention. We have to listen. That means learning to accept and embrace all of life—yes, all of it. Only then can we see it for the gift it has been. Only then can we hear the deeper song that has been singing through all of it.

All we have to do is listen…

Week 77. A Wonderful Promise

The great sage, Sri Ramana Maharshi, says if we really believe that a Higher Power guides us, then we don't need to be concerned about what happens. What a wonderful promise! This means we can let go of how we think things should be so we can be open to God's plan for us. Rather than trying to be in control, we can let the river of life take us where we are meant to go! This brings trust into play—trust in the Higher Will and the Infinite Wisdom that are always seeking to guide us.

Consciously aligning yourself with that Higher Power makes all the difference. We can't see the whole picture anyway. What we really want and what we really need are already ordained. All we have to do is let God lead us. This opens you to unimaginable creative power and brings about the best possible results in the most natural way.

Week 78. A Few Quotations from the Bible

He who rules his own spirit is mightier than he who takes a city. (Proverbs 16:32)

In quietness and confidence shall be your strength. (Isaiah 30:15)

Trust in the Lord with all your heart. In all your ways acknowledge Him and He shall direct your path. (Proverbs 3: 5-6)

Commit your way unto the Lord and trust in Him. (Psalm 37:5)

He who dwells in the secret place of the Most High shall abide under the shadow of the Almighty. (Psalm 91:1)

Week 79. Releasing Toxicity

Everything in the universe has a vibration. That vibration has a strengthening or a weakening effect. This is especially true of our thoughts and feelings. That is why we are subject to what we hold in mind.

Stress is primarily a subjective response. To a very large extent, suppressed feelings determine our stress-filled thoughts and beliefs which we then project onto the world around us. Thus the world actually becomes our mirror.

We can transcend this cycle by choosing to let go of those negative patterns and making more harmonious choices instead.

We are all doing the very best we can in any given moment. That very fact can be cause for compassion. Choosing compassion, acceptance and love for ourself and others raises us to a higher way of being, and just naturally releases the toxicity within us.

First we must become aware of the choices we are making. Then we can choose to surrender our narrow attitudes so there is room for a more expansive, more compassionate way of being.

Choices like that make all the difference.

Week 80. Healing and Wholeness

The need for healing is a call from deep within us to restore balance. We do this by becoming more attuned to our soul so God's plan can more clearly be reflected in our life.

People far wiser than I am have been saying for ages and ages that our mental life and our emotional life have a direct effect on the health of our body. Whenever there is a need for healing, just know you are getting a signal from deep within that you might need to change something. Whether that something could be a thought or an attitude, a feeling or an intention, it is up to each one of us to listen deeply so we can discern the adjustment that is needed.

"Wholeness" isn't just about "fixing" the body. It's about finding an inner balance that allows wholeness to be restored on every level.

You see, our degree of wholeness changes as we grow and evolve in our understanding. It's a lot like being in school. Once you master a certain level, you move on to the next.

Week 81. Differences

Never are differences settled by getting into the fray. Just as a problem cannot be resolved on the same level on which it occurs, so with our differences. If we are to transcend those differences, then it is necessary to take a higher view.

Doing that becomes much easier when we can humbly admit that we don't have all of the answers. When we can come from love and compassion, we begin to see more clearly.

Let us not forget that what you do to others you also do to yourself.

Week 82. The Wind in Your Sails

When questions or dilemmas or problems arise, just know that your answer is already inside you and will be revealed in a way you can clearly receive if you are listening. Sometimes guidance comes in bits and pieces. You might not get the "whole answer" all at once. Rest assured your answer is being given in just the right way, at just the right time. Learning to hear—and trust—your inner wisdom is what Deepak calls "going with the flow."

Erich Schiffman, author and master yoga instructor, calls this learning to live your daily life spontaneously, on a moment-to-moment basis, by being still inwardly and tuning in to where the life force is leading you. Then follow it, without question.

You may not know why you are going in this direction, but it feels right to you so you trust it and go with the flow. Erich says doing this frees you to fulfill a higher plan that you are not personally responsible for but which is absolutely right for you.

When you pay attention to your inner leading, a silent state of knowing happens intuitively. Whether you can explain it or not, even whether you understand it or not, you can move forward with confidence because the part of you that truly knows leaves no room for doubt.

I like to think of this way of living as having the wind in your sails. You don't know where your ship is being taken, but you can enjoy the journey because you know when you get there, that is exactly where you wanted to go.

Week 83. Living Life Consciously

We always have a choice in how we feel and how we respond to the events in our lives. Finding that out can be very freeing. I didn't know that until I was 40 years old. That realization made all the difference.

Once we begin paying attention to how we are meeting life, we begin living life consciously, instead of responding automatically, day after day. While it is certainly true that our emotions may get the upper hand sometimes, becoming aware of them begins the process of restoring balance.

If you haven't already, start paying attention to your emotions. They set the trajectory for the rest of the day—and beyond. Ask yourself—will feeling this way bring me joy? Peace? Happiness?

When you do choose, choose to be happy. Allow yourself to laugh. This does not deny the importance of what is occurring, but it does provide you with a clearer, more compassionate way of moving through it.

Week 84. When We Go Astray

Twentieth Century sage Osho tells us that sometimes life will lead us astray. Since that is a natural part of life, Osho says not to worry about it. No one can always be right. If life leads you astray, then go. He says it's okay to do that because the energy that leads you astray will also bring you back. In fact, that journey is probably part of your growth.

Osho says that whatever you did, good or bad, will prove to be the right thing because it all fits together. Then, when you look back, you wouldn't change a thing because it got you to where you presently are.

That is why Osho says to accept what is and know it isn't just part of your journey. It is your destiny.

Week 85. Inner and Outer Goals

We all have what we like to think of as inner and outer goals. When you stop to think about it, aren't we talking about the same thing? Isn't the one an expression of the other? Without that deep inner connection, everything in the outer feels hollow, empty. It doesn't really satisfy. Yet when that inner connection becomes the foundation for all that we do in the outer, a harmony and balance emerge that bring a quality to our days that could not be there without the inner as its foundation.

The one reflects the other, always. When we are grounded in our Inner Being, that truth and that essence just naturally color every aspect of our lives.

That's really the bottom line, isn't it? The deeper the well, the purer the water. When we drink from that stream, life just flows for us. Yes, and now we know—truly know—that all is well and that all shall be well because we are drinking from the stream that flows from the heart of love.

Week 86. The Essenes

We all have our own window through which we view the world, but there is another way, if we are open to it. "The Essene Gospel of Peace" suggests that we learn to see all things with the eyes of angels. What would that be like?

I'm leaving you to figure that out. That should give us all something to think about.

Week 87. Opportunity

We each have our own personal point of view, and everyone—absolutely everyone—thinks their particular view is correct. No wonder there is so much social turbulence in this world. It's as though we are looking through a knothole in a fence. What we see is accurate, given the information we have, but there is so much more.

If we can take our experiences and learn from them, they become a catalyst for our own personal growth. Isn't this what we are trying to do?

We all are growing in understanding. Our views may be different. Even though our experiences will be different, beneath it all is the One Guiding Force that is leading us in the direction of greater understanding. Yes, we are on our way, but we aren't there yet.

Therein lies the opportunity for great compassion.

Week 88. Peace and Stillness

In their essence, peace and stillness are the same thing. I don't know if you have thought about it in quite that way before. I hadn't until recently, but it makes perfect sense. I say that because when you are at peace, the mind is still. There is no anxiety, no fear, no worry. It's a lot like clear, untroubled water—no ripples, no waves, no stormy seas. Just peace—and a stillness so clear you can see into the depths of your being where you truly know that you are whole.

Week 89. One of Life's Great Lessons

Eckhart Tolle tells us that resistance is the cause of our suffering, whether it be mental, emotional or physical. I would agree.

Speaking from my own experience, resistance is a lot like anger. Whenever you bring resistance or anger into a situation, then you have two problems. You have the original problem, plus the resistance or anger.

Clarity always eludes us when we resist. We cannot see things as they are, nor can we find an acceptable resolution when we are dealing with the tension that anger and resistance engender. Learning to move beyond anger and resistance is one of life's great lessons.

Week 90. Your Inner State

What is the nature of your inner state? Happy, sad, anxious, worried, concerned? Whatever it is, that is the nature of the thought stream you are swimming in. You could even say it is the magnetic force that is propelling you in the direction you have chosen. Yes, that's right—chosen. I say that because every thought is a choice. Whatever thought you choose will bring into your life those things that are in resonance with your prevailing energy stream.

It is so easy for our thought patterns to become habitual, but that, too, is a choice. Isn't it?

Week 91. Reciprocity

No doubt you've heard the statement that every thought is a prayer. What a powerful statement! But what does that mean? How does it work?

Simply put, it means that whatever the nature of your thought is, you are asking for more of that in your life. It's the intention—the heart-felt intention—that governs the results. Here again, we are back to the concept of tuning ourselves—and thus our lives—to the highest within us.

As with us, so with our world.

Week 92. Learning to See

Your thoughts and feelings—indeed, the entirety of your life —unfolds from the timeless inner dimension within you. That is the dimension—indeed the very part of you—that knows and hears the universe singing its eternal song. This is the part of you that is always aware, the part that sees and knows.

Be that awareness and what you see will astound you. Learn to see with those eyes.

Week 93. A Simple Answer

There is an ancient metaphysical law that says we can never leave any situation that causes us discomfort until we learn to love it or at least see love at work in it. There is so much truth in that statement. Love always sets things right.

If this is true, and I believe it is, then the real work must be done within us where love and peace abide. All we have to do is stop and listen to the signals from our own internal guidance instead of just blindly plowing ahead. We begin by being still.

We are so accustomed to doing, doing, doing. It may surprise you to know that "being still" is doing something, too. (Dr. Bernie

Siegel) What are we "doing" when we are still? We are quieting our mind and body. We are listening. We are paying attention. We are moving beyond our mind to where our answers are.

In that silence, in that state of non-doing, we open the door to the understanding we have been seeking.

Week 94. A Tall Order

Whoever said, "If it costs your peace of mind, it costs too much," was right. The problem, then, is how to maintain/restore our peace of mind when we're in the middle of a muddle.

According to those far wiser than me, when we are in the midst of difficulty, the change we need begins within us. I'm talking about our perception. With how we see something. With how we choose to respond.

An ancient rishi once said, "Nothing can disturb the calm peace of my soul." When I first heard that, I wondered how that could be possible. Then I began to understand that he wasn't talking about the ego. He was talking about the part of him that really is never disturbed or upset. Perhaps that is where we need to start, too.

If we can clear our consciousness of disturbing thoughts, it becomes much easier to deepen our awareness and settle into the peace that is always present within us. Once we do that, we see with different eyes. We think with a clearer mind. When you see things differently, things are different. Why? Because whatever we see out there is simply a reflection of the level of peace we have established within us.

Getting anchored in that peace makes it much easier to accept a situation the way it is. Acceptance makes it possible to do what must be done with unconditional love.

According to my teachers, challenge is just another word for opportunity. I like that thought. If that is true, then every challenge is just another chance to practice living from our highest and best. A tall order? Yes, but it becomes far easier when we remember that what we are seeking is already within us.

Week 95. Finding A New Perspective

Life can be difficult. We all have challenges to face. We all have times when we don't know what to do. According to Dr. Bernie Siegel, when those times come, we may have to find a new way to respond, a way that may require making some internal changes in how we view things. To do that, Dr. Siegel suggests that we act like the person we want to become. Practice this new attitude. Experiment with this new way of responding to things. It may take a while for it to become our habit, but that's ok. As Bernie's mother often told him, "Fake it until you make it."

The surprising thing is, when we do establish a new way of being, answers we were seeking just show up spontaneously.

They were there all along, of course. We just had to clear the way for them to appear.

Week 96. Being Ordinary

If you're at all like me, you've probably had times when you've had the blahs. Life seemed ordinary. Whatever you were doing didn't seem to have any particular meaning or purpose.

The good news, according to Dr. David Hawkins, is that just being ordinary is an expression of divinity!

As I was thinking about how this might be true, I happened to walk by the Lilies of the Valley in my garden. They are so small. So inconspicuous. So ordinary. Yet when I got to examining them closely, I was amazed at how special—how delicate—how fragrant—they are. "Maybe being ordinary," I thought to myself, "isn't so ordinary after all."

Dr. Hawkins agrees. He says we can discover our own truth through everyday life. More than that, he promises that to live with care and kindness is all that is necessary. The rest will just naturally reveal itself when the time is right.

I love that thought! Wouldn't it be wonderful if caring and kindness were so common that they were ordinary, too? What a difference that would make! And we can do that! We all can do that! It's simply a matter of choice.

Thank you, Dr. Hawkins—again.

Week 97. Your Heart Knows

As I am sure you already know, the mind likes to chatter—constantly. There are times when that's ok. It helps release stress. However, when we are looking for answers, when we have a decision to make, when something important comes up and we need to know what to do, we won't find our answers in all that chatter. Those are the times when we need to go beyond our mind and tap into our own deep inner wisdom.

When you meditate regularly, then you learn how to silence your mind. If you don't yet know how to meditate, then try telling your mind to be still. Talk to it like you would talk to a child. "That's enough. Be still." Then shift your awareness to a state of no thought. If that seems difficult, don't give up. The more you do it, the easier it gets.

When you need to make a decision, when you need an answer, ask your question and then shift into your silent mode. Let the answer surface in its own way and its own time. It might not come immediately, but when it does come, you will know in your heart that it is right.

Your silent state is where your answers are. More than that, it's where your truth resides.

Week 98. Getting Out of the Way

Betty Eadie says being led by faith is more important than being led by knowledge. She is right. When we are led by knowledge, we are limited by what we think we know. When we are led by faith, when we trust in the unknown, we are open to infinite possibilities.

There is a Higher Wisdom and a Higher Plan within those possibilities where everything has a purpose and everything is under control. As I write this, the words "Divine Order" come to mind.

Strange as it may seem, when we do trust in Divine Order, we are guided by a Higher Wisdom. Yes, and we begin to see that everything really is fulfilling a higher purpose, whether it may seem like it or not.

Amazing, isn't it...

Week 99. The Ultimate Purpose

There is an over-arching purpose to your life that far exceeds in importance anything you might be doing "out here" on the material plane. While your goals, ambitions and desires certainly have their importance, their place in the ultimate scheme of things has more to do with how they contribute to your own personal spiritual growth and understanding.

We all have dreams we hope to actualize, yet there are many people for whom that actualization never happens. That is why it's important to know that life is always taking you in the direction you are meant to go for your own spiritual growth.

Making peace with this great truth becomes possible when you can accept the fact that you are never in control of your life. True, the dreams and goals and ambitions are still there, but it is important to remember that while the intention is yours, the result is not up to you.

How much better it is to trust the Hand that is steering your ship. Then you can know that however things work out, they are always for your highest good.

Week 100. How Gandhi Overcame Anger

When I was growing up, we were very much aware of what Gandhi was doing on the other side of the planet. We would see him in the news reels at the theaters (TV hadn't been thought of yet and movies were fairly new). We would hear him on the radio and read about him in the newspapers. What he said and what he did shone like a beacon clear over here and left an impression in my young heart that never left me.

If you don't know much about Gandhi, I recommend Eknath Easwaran's excellent book, *Gandhi, the Man*. It will give you a good idea of the intentional inner transformation Gandhi underwent to eliminate anger and hostility from his personality.

You see, anger had become his habitual response, but Gandhi was determined to eliminate that habit. He succeeded by continually replacing his anger with what he did want—each and every day.

This practice, this inner work, is how the nonviolent movement that freed India from British domination was born. It all began with one person whose diligent inner work changed everything.

How did Gandhi do this? Whenever he was struggling with negative emotions, Gandhi would go for a quick walk. With every step he would repeat his favorite name for God. Soon this would bring the rhythm of his walk and the rhythm of his breathing in sync, with the rhythm of his thinking following soon after. Over the years, this practice gradually reached into Gandhi's deepest layers and brought him a sense of peace that nothing could shake.

According to Gandhi, this practice can carry us through every ordeal. It may sound simple, but if you are in doubt, just try it. See for yourself the discipline it requires—and the difference it can make. Just choose a word or a phrase to focus on. You could use your favorite name for God, as Gandhi did, or it could be an attribute you'd like to strengthen within yourself. It could even be an affirmation or a Bible verse that really speaks to you. Whatever you choose, be consistent so the effect of its vibration can become established deep within you. Then, whenever you are struggling with something, do as Gandhi did. Just start where you are, and don't give up.

One thing you may notice as you do this is that your thinking process may slow down. This is definitely good news. Why? Because the more control you have over your mind, the more control you have over your life.

Week 101. Nuggets of Gold

We've all had times when we were pressed to the max by situations or circumstances that came into our lives. While we would never have asked for these things to happen, when we look back later, we can see what we learned and how we grew through it.

What I find so interesting is that the resources we are looking for almost always are within us. That inner wisdom is like a seed that is just waiting for its time to bloom.

Quite some time ago Dr. Bernie Siegel said we can be free of our pain. Why? Because we are the solution! When I first heard that, I had just lost my husband, with both parents soon to follow. How do you free yourself of pain like that?

Well, you don't. Not right away, but it can happen. Given time. Perhaps even years—years of deep introspection, prayer, searching, and all that goes with it—to bring that inner wisdom and deep understanding to the surface.

The only way this can happen is if we are willing to do the work. It is by tilling our inner field that we learn to accept what has happened. Acceptance is key. Whatever has happened is part of life, and there is no changing that.

Deepak says our most difficult situations oftentimes reveal our deepest truths. This tells me there are nuggets of gold hidden in every situation. When we find them, we also find meaning, and perhaps even a purpose, behind it all. In that discovery is the beginning of peace.

Week 102. When Your Meditation Becomes Your Life

I made an interesting discovery the other day. I'd gone to the bank to get something out of my safe deposit box and the banker wouldn't let me open it. She said there was a problem with one of the signatures. I won't go into the entire conversation. I'll simply say that the corrected signature had been entered two years ago, and the bank forgot to post it. In the meantime, this very pleasant young woman was calling department after department, trying to see if she could get clearance to let me open my box while I was sitting there watching the clock go around and around. I could feel myself getting tense. Irritated. You probably know the feeling.

I knew I needed to choose a healthier response. I could see I was trying to control something that was out of my hands. Slow deep breathing helped but it wasn't the whole answer. Then I remembered what that ancient sage said so long ago: "Nothing can disturb the calm peace of my soul." Immediately I shifted to that place deep inside me where there was no turmoil, and my inner climate changed radically.

This potentially frustrating situation became an opportunity to practice what I thought I knew. What it taught me was—when meditation becomes your practice, your life becomes your meditation!

I'd never thought about it in quite that way before, and I had to smile. Lately we've been talking about when your life becomes your meditation. Well, there it is. Applying the principles can indeed be a meditation. Doing that makes all the difference.

Week 103. Learning to Surf

One of the first things I did after my husband's sudden death nearly 30 years ago was go to the book store. I needed help and I needed it badly, so I brought home a stack of books and read and read, searching for the answers I so desperately needed.

That's when I came across Dr. Jon Kabat-Zinn's wonderful observation: "You can't stop the waves, but you can learn to surf." (*Wherever You Go, There You Are*)

That really got my attention. It hadn't yet occurred to me that there was something I could do about the awful anguish I was feeling. That thought became my life-raft as I moved through the stormy seas that had engulfed me.

Quite often, when upsetting things come into our lives, it can feel a lot like we are at the mercy of the circumstances we are facing. That could not be farther from the truth. We always have a choice in how we respond. Knowing that doesn't mean it will easy. We may still have to ride the emotional roller coaster we are on for a while, and that's okay. The important thing is to recognize that nothing lasts forever. No matter how difficult something may seem, if we just keep moving forward, eventually the waves will subside and we will find ourselves on the other side of all of that distress.

All the more reason to ride the waves as best you can when they do come. Peace is always waiting on the other side.

Week 104. Suffering and Compost

In his book, Michael Ciborski compares suffering to compost. He has a good point, because suffering does become the soil out of which much learning comes. Then he reminds us that we can grow roses in compost! After all, without compost, no flowers! What a lovely way to put a positive slant to things that can be so difficult.

Rainer Maria Rilke must have known this when he suggested that we trust in the difficult. It is through the difficult that we are given a chance to learn something important.

When those tough times come, trust the forces that are at work in your life. Everything is unfolding exactly the way it is supposed to, whether it seems like it or not.

Year Three

Week 105. Kindness

For most of us, being kind is our natural intention, but what about those times when someone does something that doesn't seem very kind to us? At that moment, we are being given a choice. We can either respond in like measure, or we can choose to be kind.

We may not know what prompted the other person's behavior. What we do know is that we are being given an opportunity to offer kindness where it is needed. That choice allows love to come into the situation, which is probably what is needed most in that particular moment.

It is in moments like these that kindness becomes our practice. If it truly is our practice, it becomes our habit. This is where conscious living comes in. Paying attention to what we think and what we do and say always leads to the best possible outcome—not just for ourselves, but for others, too.

According to Eknath Easwaran, our real job is to be kind. Then, no matter where we are or what we are doing, we will be true to our high calling.

When we remember to come from our highest and best, no matter what the circumstances, all are blessed.

Week 106. Surrender

When there is complete trust, there is no fear. We don't feel the need to control. We just trust. If you have ever watched a baby asleep in the arms of its mother, then you know what I mean.

There is a love that holds us like that mother. That love keeps us completely safe, with no need to worry or fear. We can rest in that love just like the child in its mother's arms. We can trust that love. We can trust it completely. This is not to say life will not have its difficult moments, but when we trust that loving presence completely, when we trust with all our heart, then we know that whatever life brings us, love is still at work in our lives.

Love ever and always wants us to trust so much that it does not matter what happens "out here." Then our only thought is one of trust and abiding love.

That is the purpose of surrender. Surrender allows the Divine to have its way with us, no matter what. We can do that, because in our heart we know we are safe. We know we are secure. We know we are loved.

Week 107. The Promise

Here I am, on the eastern side of Nebraska, where two-thirds of our counties are either under water or surrounded by water. This could well be the worst flood on record for our part of the Midwest. Lives and livelihoods are being changed forever.

While we are literally trying to keep afloat here in eastern Nebraska, ranchers in the northwest part of our state were hit by a massive blizzard that has given them no choice but to dig their cattle out of the snow that has all but covered them up. How does one find a sense of stability in the midst of this kind of chaos?

Life is always calling us to go deeper, and that is certainly true for those of us here in the Midwest. We may never know the "why" of our circumstances, but we will always know Who we can lean on.

The promise is, "I will not forsake you." (Isaiah 41:17)

If we truly believe that, then wouldn't trust be our natural, faith-filled response?

Week 108. God's Timing

About a year ago, a dear friend brought me a blooming succulent. I've always been fascinated by succulents, but never had any success keeping them.

The directions that came with this plant said to give it only two ice cubes a week. Even though that seemed rather odd, I decided to give it a try. About six months later I noticed little green shoots at the end of the stems. I'm talking about maybe 1/16" of new green. I was quite surprised at the sign of new life, so I kept on giving it two ice cubes a week. Then one day, after about nine months, I noticed two buds on one of the stems. I decided I must be doing something right, even if I didn't know what it was.

Well, we are at the one-year mark now, and this morning I was greeted with such a delicate little blossom that all I could do was stand and gaze at it. For some strange reason, it didn't matter to this little plant that it was 12 below zero here this week. It didn't matter that we were in the dead of winter. It was ready to bloom, and bloom it did.

Nature is so eloquent. In her own way, she tells us to just wait, be patient. If we knew why something seems to take so long, we wouldn't want to rush the process. God's timing is always beyond our understanding.

Whenever things aren't going the way you want them to, just know that Wisdom is at work here. Whatever you are waiting for will come in its own time, and that will always be the perfect time.

Week 109. A Light We Cannot See

The past few days I've been watching the orchid plant I told you about last week because it had a second bud that was getting ready to bloom.

This morning I was really surprised to see that it had indeed opened. What was amazing to me was that it opened during the night! I always thought flowers opened to the light. If that is true, then this little orchid opened to a light we cannot see.

I find this so inspiring! Why? Because if this little orchid can bloom in the dark, we can, too! I find great comfort in that thought. I hope you will, too.

Week 110. Opposites

It is so easy to get caught up in all the opposites life presents us. We like to think in terms of right or wrong, good or bad, dark or light, up or down. Those polarities just seem to go with the territory, and in a way they do. However, there is another approach that changes how all of those opposites color our lives. Buddha called it "the middle way." Jesus said it more simply: "Be still." But what were they saying?

Have you ever noticed how a clock's pendulum is always swinging back and forth, from one extreme to the other? That's what we do, too, when we bounce back and forth between those polarities. But what happens when the pendulum stops? It is still. That is what Jesus was talking about. He asks us to rest in being. Not judging. Not choosing. Just being.

When you are quiet, it gets easier to hear your deep wisdom and sense where your heart is leading you. It gets easier to see how—ultimately—everything is simply a movement of the love that is behind it all.

The mind thinks in terms of duality, of opposites. It wants to understand. Your spirit doesn't do that. Your spirit just is. In that

Is-ness is a love that is beyond all the opposites. That love is silent, and it is deeper than your mind can ever go.

Once you experience that love, once you realize that love is the truth of your being, the problem of dealing with opposites just falls away.

Week 111. Intentions

It is so important to keep your inner speech in line with your intentions because, as Wayne Dyer reminds us, your inner voice will <u>always</u> win. Why? Because you are only subject to what you hold in your mind! (Dr. David Hawkins)

You can't expect to get orange juice if all you have are apples. The same is true of your intentions. You can't expect your intentions to materialize if you undermine them through your thinking. When you support your intentions by how you think and feel, then Spirit collaborates with you. (Dyer again)

What more could one ask?

Week 112. Life's Lessons

No doubt by now you've heard the saying, "We are not human beings trying to have a spiritual experience. We are spiritual beings having a human experience."

For many of us, changing from the first view to the second view involves a shift in our perception. That shift oftentimes comes through growth and expansion of our understanding. Making that shift is a lot like planting a seed and waiting for it to grow. When the conditions are right, the seed will grow and bear fruit. True of plants, true of us.

When a new concept comes along and you're willing to give it serious thought, possibly even embrace it and try to shape your life so it reflects that truth, you are nurturing a seed that has been planted.

The problems we experience in life always offer opportunities for growth. When the same problem keeps repeating itself, that simply means the lesson is still waiting to be learned. Once we "get" the lesson, we move on to other lessons.

When we do the necessary inner work, we outgrow our problems. It's a lot like moving from arithmetic to algebra.

The lessons may not get easier, but they do make us stronger.

Week 113. True Prosperity

The Atacama Desert in Chili, South America, is one of the driest places on the planet. There are parts of this desert that never ever receive any moisture. While such an environment would seem uninhabitable to most of us, there are oases here and there where people actually thrive. They grow fruit and vegetables and raise horses, sheep and goats. These small communities usually have no more than ten families, yet these people are very happy. They live simple lives in peace and harmony with each other and with their environment.

Not long ago, when a researcher was traveling in this area, he came across a young man who raises horses, just as his ancestors have been doing for a very long time. The young man loved what he was doing and was content with how he was living his life.

The researcher asked him how he could be so happy when he had so little. "When you love what you are doing," the young man replied, "you have everything you want."

Wise words indeed!

Week 114. Freedom

Freedom is definitely an inside job. No matter what we'd like to be free from, or free to do, being free always begins within us.

You'd like more peace in your life? The only place peace can happen is within you.

You'd like to feel better physically? The only place healing can begin is within you.

You'd like to feel happy? Happiness always begins within us. True happiness—true joy—never depends on something outside us.

Yes, we may need to ask someone for help along the way—thank Goodness for our way-showers! That doesn't change the fact that the work is still ours to do.

We all have to find the way to our own freedom/happiness/joy/peace/wellbeing. The beauty of it is that when we do the work, when we do find what we are looking for, no one can take it away from us. Not ever.

Week 115. Questions

Since it seems like there will always be questions, I'm wondering if it might be possible to just let the questions be questions. Eventually, when I am ready, they will lead me to answers. In the meantime, I think I'll just live with them. I'll turn them over and examine them like leaves in the Fall. Which ones are worth keeping, which should be discarded? Which ones am I comfortable enough to live with for a while? Do I really want them in my garden? If they were to bear fruit, would I be pleased?

That is the gift time gives us. Time to consider. Time to choose. If the answers came too quickly, we might find we didn't want them after all. Or worse yet, we might not be ready.

Two things have to happen before answers come: the question has to be right, and we must be ready for the answer. That being the case, I guess I'll just be content to grow at whatever pace life allows, knowing there is a higher wisdom that is directing it all.

Week 116. Being Perfect

For years and years I tried to be perfect. It just didn't work. I finally gave up and decided doing my best was all I could manage. Oh yes, I still made mistakes, yet even those mistakes were the best I could do at the time. I didn't realize that then, but I do now.

The other day I came across a statement by Thich Nhat Hahn about trying to be perfect that I'd like to pass along to you, because I can't help thinking I'm not the only one who has struggled with this.

Hahn says we shouldn't worry about being perfect. He says we are meant to be whole, so just be yourself.

If you ever needed permission—there it is.

Week 117. Loving Yourself

This topic is one many of us aren't comfortable with. We've been taught to think about others so much that we may have forgotten how to care about ourself. If this is true for you, what we're talking about isn't all that complicated. Maybe you could start with something really easy. Maybe you could listen to your body and pay attention to what it says. After all, your body knows what you really need, and it always speaks in language that is easy to understand—comfort or discomfort, for example.

Something else you could do is make sure that your needs are being met—whether they are physical, mental, emotional or spiritual. That would mean really paying attention, wouldn't it?

Why is this so important? Because you can't offer others what you don't yet have yourself. As I've said many times, you have to take care of yourself if you want to be able to give out of your fullness, instead of your dregs.

When you are doing all of the above, then you are being true to yourself. You are doing what you know is kind and right and honorable. Isn't that what loving yourself (and others) means?

I know that can seem like a lot if you've been running yourself ragged. If that is where you are right now, just choose one thing and start there. Just focus on whatever is calling to you the most. What do you really need right now?

We all have to begin somewhere. Why not there?

Week 118. Chaos

Too often, when life gets hectic, we get thrown off center, but it doesn't have to be that way. If there is chaos, then let there be chaos. The important thing to remember is that the chaos is not you. As Deepak has said many times, when there is chaos, the universe is just re-arranging things. Your part is simply to stay in the eye of the storm. Even though chaos may be happening all around you, absolutely nothing is happening to you. Why? Because you are the silent center, so drop your anchor there and peacefully ride out whatever is happening. This really is possible!

Just remember—you are the peace, not the chaos. That simple shift of attention makes all the difference. As the ancient sages often said, "Nothing can disturb the calm peace of my soul."

It was true for them, it's true for you.

Week 119. An Affirmation

Many years ago I came across the following affirmation: There is only one Presence and one Power at work in my life—God, the Good, Omnipotent.

If you really believe this, then you know that whatever comes into your life is there to lead you into a deeper knowledge—and yes, a deeper relationship—with the Presence in which you live, and move, and have your being. If you truly understand that, you also know that ultimately all things are rooted in Love.

Need I say more?

Week 120. A Dichotomy

Unbeknownst to me, my email carrier was making changes that prevented me from sending out some of my messages. When I called to ask about it, I was given detailed instructions on how I could fix the problem. I did my best to do that. When the emails still wouldn't send, I called the company again and found out they

71

were still working on the changes. They said it would probably be fixed yet that week, but it wasn't. Since I couldn't talk to them on Saturday, there I was with the problem unresolved.

Situations like this have always been difficult for me. Since I didn't want to let it spoil my day, I put the whole issue on the back burner until Monday in the hope that I could get some answers then.

While this didn't make the problem go away, it left me in a rather unusual space. I say that because there was a part of me that was very much at peace, and there was a part of me that wasn't. I don't recall ever having a dichotomy as clearly evident in my life. It's an odd feeling— having peace and agitation equally present. It's rather like mixing oil and water—and being neither. So what are you when you are neither?

Week 121. Expectations

Back in 2000, when I was preparing to go to India with Deepak for the first time, my mind was filled with anxious questions. What about the water? Malaria? The food? Etc!

When I got to the annual teachers' retreat in July, I saw other teachers had the same concerns. Once Deepak saw where we were coming from, he just sat back and smiled. Then he said something I've never forgotten—and it applies to every moment of our lives: "Well, the first thing you need to know is your experience will match your expectations."

What a wake-up call that was! At least it was for me. "I'd better shape up!" was my first thought. Hearing that was a quantum shift for me. I've tried to practice that principle ever since, and do you know what I've found? He was right, of course.

Week 122. Opening the Door

Each one of us is a unique creation. Whether that uniqueness has the opportunity to reach its full maturity is dependent to a very large extent on the choices we make, the aspirations we pursue, the meanings and values we cherish. That, and our willingness to let God mold and shape us according to His unerring design, frees us to discover who and what we are meant to be at our highest and best. The key, then, at least as I see it, is to seek to know and do God's Will in all things.

When you open that door, it never closes.

Week 123. Invisible Magnets

We live in a sea of thoughts, and they are streaming around us all the time. Like dust in the air, thoughts are always "out there" because they are part of the global consciousness.

While not every thought that comes into your head belongs to you, it will become your thought if you engage with it.

Thoughts are like magnets. When a thought becomes part of your inner conversation, you can be sure similar thoughts will fill your mind. They'll draw more of the same to themselves. If you aren't careful, those thoughts become a pattern, and patterns become an attitude. They become a habitual way of moving through life.

This is why it is so important to choose your thoughts. As I told someone just the other day, thoughts are like guests. You don't invite everyone who knocks on your door to come in. It is the same with our thoughts. If you don't want that kind of energy working in your life, then don't engage with the thought. It's that simple.

"Simple" things are not always easy—but they are possible.

Week 124. Your Testimony

One of the things life has been teaching me is that all things can be used for some good purpose. God doesn't waste a single moment of our lives—even when our lives are a mess. Max Lucado says that mess will eventually become your message. And when you feel you are being tested in some way? Again, Lucado says that test will eventually become your testimony.

You see, whatever is going on in your life isn't just about you. How you meet your challenges becomes a silent testimony that says far more than words ever can.

Whenever you are working through something, just know you are being given a gift—and the gift isn't just for you.

Week 125. There Is Nothing to Fear

When we move into the silence of meditation, we enter into that inner space where there are no boundaries, where there is only peace, and all is well. If we really understood that, we would know that everything is exactly as it should be, even when it doesn't seem that way.

It isn't easy to look beyond what seems apparent to the underlying truth—our very Reality even—which we cannot see with our human eyes but which we can experience in the silence of our heart. That is what we must learn to do if we are ever to find the peace we are seeking. Indeed, the peace is already within us.

There is a line by an unknown author that says, "Pray not against fear, but for understanding, for when the Truth is known, you will know there is nothing to fear." And so it is.

Week 126. Perspective

One of my favorite quotes from Deepak is, "When things don't happen the way I expect, I trust that I don't have the bigger picture." I can't count the times I've fallen back on that thought when life wasn't going the way I thought it would. Then the other day I came across a thought by Rumi with a slightly different slant: "Some things that don't happen keep disasters from occurring."

Either way you look at it, those are pretty good reasons to just go with the flow and trust that "Something" knows what is supposed to happen, whether we do or not.

Week 127. Stormy Weather

There was a time in my life when it seemed as though I was living on a raging sea. My little boat was constantly being buffeted by great surging waves. It was all I could do to keep afloat. Perhaps you've had times like that, too.

It took a long time—or at least it seemed like a long time—for me to find out that beneath all of my raging storms, there was only stillness and a beauty that would be impossible to describe. This is true for all of us. Whenever we encounter storms and challenges on the surface of our lives, below that raging sea there is only peace.

Where we place our anchor makes all the difference. As long as my anchor was in shallow water, it was of no help at all. It was only when I began to sink my anchor into deeper waters that I discovered it was possible to ride those difficult currents without being overcome by them.

In *Full Catastrophe Living*, Dr. Jon Kabat Zinn says we can't stop the waves from coming, but we can learn to surf. That is exactly what we are doing when we meditate. We are learning to surf.

The next time a challenge comes your way, do remember to check and see how deeply you are setting your anchor. It can make all the difference.

Week 128. It's All Perfect

Dr. David Hawkins says everything is perfect just the way it is. A bud is a perfect bud, a flower in bloom is a perfect flower in bloom, and a withered flower is a perfect withered flower.

If we translate that so it refers to us, then everything is perfect just the way it is for us, too. Although things may not be the way we'd like them to be, they are perfect the way they are because they are what we need at that moment as we continue to grow and evolve.

As Shunryu Suzuki has often said, even though everything is perfect just the way it is, there is still a lot of room for improvement.

I hope you smiled when you read that. I know I did.

Week 129. We Are Never Alone

Rumi tells us the moon stays bright because it doesn't avoid the night. Faith is like that moon. It guides us through the dark and shows us the way. The way is always here. We can't always see it, but we can trust in its presence.

I love watching the moon. Every time I see it, I am reminded of the beautiful anthem that says, "He, watching over Israel, slumbers not nor sleeps."*

No matter how dark the way, we are never truly alone.

*From Mendelssohn's *Elijah* (Psalm 121:4)

Week 130. An Encouraging Thought

Even as a small child, I always liked to plan ahead, yet more times than I could count, those plans never happened. "Life" had other ideas. Sometimes I welcomed the change, many times I didn't. I think that is how it is for most of us, don't you?

Being able to accept what comes with an open heart does make it easier to go with the constant flux of life. While that isn't always easy to do, Bishop TD Jakes says whatever seems to be working against you is actually working for you.

He is right, of course.

Week 131. The River and the Sea

No doubt you've heard the expression that the river always finds the sea, but have you ever wondered how the river even knows where the sea is? There must be something that keeps moving it toward its ultimate destination.

I think we are a lot like that. Our highest ideals call to us just as the sea calls to the river. We may not hear that call. We may not even feel its call, but it is drawing us toward itself, whether we know it or not.

Reaching the sea isn't something you do. Getting there happens quietly, in its own way. You could even say reaching the sea is our destiny. We can't take any credit for that movement, that growth. It is the result of our own inner call.

Follow the light within you. Live your truth, and life will take you where you are destined to go.

Week 132. Learning to Choose

It is so easy to get caught up in negativity, criticism and judgment, even when we know such choices will pull us down. If we aren't careful, those responses can become a habit.

How can we avoid that trap? How can we bring more peace and joy into our lives when there is negativity is all around us?

According to Dr. David Hawkins, the answer lies in whether or not we choose to allow something to upset us. We can choose to harbor "bad" feelings. We can choose to respond in like kind. What to do? Choose the opposite! It may not be easy, especially at first, but it is possible.

Make that your practice. When there is anger or dissension, choose love. Choose to forgive. You can refuse to let negative feelings enter your heart. When you read or hear about potentially disquieting events, choose not to judge. Instead, choose to trust that God is working His purposes out.

We can always choose to trust the Higher Will. Our Creator always has our best interests at heart.

Week 133. Limitations and Possibilities

Dr. David Hawkins tells us our limitations do not define us. They imply possibilities. They show us where our potential for growth is.

When I was learning arithmetic, I didn't even know algebra existed, yet the day did come when I understood algebra enough to integrate its principles into my life.

While that is a rather simple example, it does show us how what we tend to think of as a limitation is really a signpost. It shows us "where growth is imminent," as author John O'Donohue has said. I like that thought. Growth is always imminent.

When those moments come along where you feel stuck, or stymied, or limited, or just plain challenged, please know you have found a place in your life where there is potential for growth. That growth can take you to places you never ever dreamed of.

Deepak suggests we "dare to go where there is no path and leave a trail." Why not?

Week 134. Why Do We Meditate?

For many of us, when we first want to learn how to meditate, we don't really know what we are looking for. All we know is we want to be more calm. We want to handle stress better. We want to be more attuned to our own spirituality. So we start shopping. We try this technique, then that one, seldom settling into a solid practice because we haven't yet found what we were looking for.

That is where I was when I found a practice that really interested me. I felt different when I did it. I began to see things in a new way. I wasn't as easily upset, and I wondered why.

When a practice is right for you, it's a lot like turning a key in a lock. It opens you to a higher vibration, a clearer perspective, a truer understanding. It's a lot like looking at life from a higher elevation, like standing on a mountain and viewing the plains. How we see things changes completely. That shift is a sign of Grace. When you reach up, Grace meets you and helps you in your climb.

If you are faithful in your practice, that higher "view" establishes itself and life begins to flow for you. That doesn't mean you won't have difficult days. What it does mean is that even on the difficult days, you are still anchored in the knowledge that you are ok, regardless of what is going on.

This shift in how you live your life is when your spirit really starts to wake up. Instead of letting habitual responses run your life, you've begun choosing your thoughts and actions.

As you begin living life with greater awareness, your days become more in sync with the Higher Plan. You begin to move beyond what you were as you grow into what you can be—not deliberately, but naturally, normally, all as a result of "tuning in" to the Inner Presence you've come to know during your faithful practice of meditation.

You see, you don't close the world out when you meditate. Instead, you open yourself to what you and your world can be. That is just the beginning of where meditation can take you.

Week 135. Your Soul Always Knows

Years ago when my husband and I were driving up the Maine seacoast, we found some enchanting side roads that took us to quaint little places. We enjoyed just following our noses, and we did that for most of the day until we noticed the sun was getting low in the sky. We knew if we didn't get back on the main road, we wouldn't have a place to stay that night.

We had to scramble a bit, but as chance would have it, we got the last room available in that area. It was up a narrow staircase above a very old inn and restaurant. We were grateful for a place to sleep, even though we had to be careful not to hit our heads on the saltbox ceiling just above us.

If we hadn't wandered the way we did, we would have missed a lot of the charm of that New England seacoast. I'm glad we took the long way, even though we had to scramble for a place to sleep.

In *The Only Thing That Matters*, Neale Donald Walsch tells us that going the long way is not the same as going the wrong way. He also says the short way isn't always faster either. There is a lot of truth in both of those statements. Many times the lessons we really need can only be found when we get off the main road, when we take the long way. On the other hand, the short way can be truly challenging, too.

I guess what it boils down to is that we are always going to meet what we need to meet so we can grow in the ways we need to grow.

Even though those times can be challenging, there is much for which we can be thankful, and here is the reason why—our Soul always knows where we are going. It also knows why.

Week 136. Trust

Many years ago I had the opportunity to ride a hydrofoil across the North Sea from Denmark to Sweden. I'll never forget standing in the front of the boat, face into the wind, much like those figures you see on ancient ships. It was a timeless moment, one where I felt connected to something much deeper than myself. It left me with the feeling that no matter what happens, Something is carrying me across the waters of my life.

I leaned heavily on that memory nearly 30 years ago when my life changed drastically. I had no idea how to proceed. I was overwhelmed. I felt lost. Utterly lost. It was a moment of deep surrender.

As with all times of surrender, when I let go—completely let go—guidance came. That guidance changed my life. Not only did it offer me new meaning and purpose for my life, it brought what I had always been looking for and didn't know how to find.

Sometimes the only way we can really touch upon that deep Wisdom is by going through those great upheavals.

We all have tough times. No one is exempt. When those times do come, trust in the unseen Hand that is guiding you. It always knows the way.

Week 137. When Great Crises Come

Dr. David Hawkins tells us that our limited, individual self cannot handle the "overwhelm" that oftentimes accompanies traumatic life events. Yet there is something greater than our personal self that is more than able to handle those difficult times. That is why these experiences are so valuable.

The mind wants to cling to what is familiar but at times of great crisis, the familiar isn't there anymore. The only way through the situation is to let go completely. When we can do that, we discover there is a Power within us which is greater than our personal self. That Power is able to sustain us, no matter what.

Eventually, the willingness to surrender to that Guidance becomes a lifestyle. We begin doing this on a daily basis. It becomes our attitude. Our whole approach to life changes, all because we've learned to depend on a Presence that is more than able to handle whatever comes up.

When I look back on my own life-changing events, it was like everything had shifted. I was in a new place, a different place, and I had absolutely no conscious idea of how to proceed. Even so, there was "Something" that did know. In surrendering to that Wisdom, I found both the answers I was seeking and the way I needed to go.

We all have an Inner Guide. When those times come, trust in your Inner Wisdom. Let go and let it lead you. There is a reason for whatever you are working through, and it is deeper than you presently know.

Week 138. Storms

When Gandhi said he loved storms, he wasn't talking about a winter blizzard. He was referring to the inner turmoil we sometimes experience as we move through life. While it may not seem like it at the time, storms like that can be quite productive. They give us a chance to learn something about ourself. They teach us things we might not learn any other way.

Storms like that can take us places we would rather not go. While they may stretch us to the limit, they can also be our greatest teachers.

When you can walk through storms that totally turn your life upside down and come out wiser, perhaps even stronger, the day does come when you can look back and feel grateful not only for what you have learned, but that you were able to come through it all and feel even more whole.

While we may not have known it at the time, we were being guided and protected every step of the way. Truth is, we never walk that road alone.

Week 139. The Power of Thought

If you aren't already familiar with Dr. Masaru Emoto's book, *The Messages from Water*, then do take a look. What you find may surprise you.

The book (actually this is the first in a series) is filled with amazing pictures of the changes water makes when exposed to outside influences, particularly thought. He shows how even crystals change according to the kind of energy around them. You'll get to see what chlorinated water looks like, as well as water from various cities and the effects of pollution on their water. He shows us how beautiful water is when it is pure, as well as how thoughts, words or intentions affect and change the water. He has even played music to water and shows us how music can either heal or "injure" the water. In some of his experiments, he puts printed words under glasses of water to see if there is a difference. There is, to an amazing extent.

His is a fascinating book, very thought-provoking and should give us cause for thought. I say this because our body is mostly water. This means that our thoughts, our feelings, what we consume, even our environment all contribute to the health of our body. Even though most of us already know this, I'm guessing that few of us have had the opportunity to actually see the difference these factors make in such a startlingly clear way.

If we've never taken these things seriously, we should. As the old saying goes, seeing is believing. Well, here is a chance to see for yourself. It would be time well spent.

Week 140. Detours

If you've been driving around the city lately, as have I, no doubt you've encountered unexpected detours. You thought you were going to go this way, only to find out you have to go that way instead. As that happened to me—again—yesterday, I couldn't help thinking how like life that is. We're just toodling along, thinking we have everything under control, when suddenly life takes an unexpected turn and life changes completely. It would be easy to get upset, even angry, at this change in our plans.

Eventually the time does come when we have to say, ok, this is how it is. How can I move forward from here?

There is always a Way. Although we may not know what that Way is right now, it is here, just waiting for us.

Sometimes we just have to go a step at a time. When we do, we may not even realize we are on a Path because all we can see is this one step. That's where Trust comes into the picture. Trust the Hand that is guiding you, that is showing you this one step. Other steps will follow, of that we can be sure. We may not be able to see those other steps right now, but they will be there.

Eventually you will be able to look back and see how you got to where you currently are. You'll see the path you followed, how it unfolded a step at a time, and you'll marvel at the Wisdom that was always guiding you.

You see, we are never lost. Not even in our darkest moments. There is always a Way.

Week 141. Talk to Your Body

The first time someone suggested that I talk to my body, I wasn't sure I'd heard correctly. "What did you say?" was my reply, but that was exactly what he said.

I have since learned that our body is like a child in that we take care of it, we nourish it and we try to do what is best for it so it can do what it knows how to do most efficiently.

83

Everyone likes to be appreciated. Your body does, too. Have you ever said "thank you" to your body, or praised it for the good job it is doing?

Years ago the children in our church did an experiment where some of them talked to their plants while other children didn't. The difference after a month was amazing. What I didn't know then was that your body is like that, too. It appreciates your praise and encouragement and appreciation. When your body hurts, it appreciates being comforted.

You can even sing to your body! Yes, I said sing. Soft and gentle humming (that's called toning) can be very soothing to your body.

If you haven't ever done this, I suggest you try it. If you aren't comfortable saying "thank you" out loud, you can always whisper it or even just think it.

Your body responds to your every thought. That's a good thing to know, because if you haven't been paying attention to your thoughts, now would be a very good time to begin.

Week 142. Unseen Blessings

I've been saying for quite some time—perhaps you have been thinking this, too—that every bit of progress we make lifts the whole. Nothing you do is for yourself alone. The same love connects us all.

Andrew Harvey says no awakening can be personal or selfish. The love that grows within us is like light—it spreads everywhere, blessing all it touches.

Surely the Sri Lankan saint Bawa Muhaiyaddeen must have known this. He didn't get caught up in points of view, or who was right and who was wrong. Life was much simpler for him. Instead, love was his religion. For him, love was a way of life.

We can be like that, too. As we hold to the course and remain constant in our love for all beings, everything changes. It would have to. Nothing would be untouched. If the only prayer we make is to become that light, that love, someone somewhere will find the going a little easier, their courage a little stronger, their hope a little brighter.

As Dr. David Hawkins once said, when the sea rises, so do all the ships upon it. That is exactly what happens when you offer that kind word, that loving thought, that helping hand.

Truly, we are in this together.

Week 143. Trials

A guest speaker at church recently said the trials we encounter in life are like course work. They contain lessons we can't get any other way. Once we get through one lesson, that doesn't mean we are done learning. He assured us there will always be a next level.

He also promised that whether we know where life is taking us or not, God knows the plans. Regardless of the difficulty, we can rest assured that God is always our eternal Guide.

Hearing that was rather like a breath of fresh air for me. I hope so for you, too.

Week 144. Truth

Dr. David Hawkins talks a lot about how truth is true at the level at which it is understood, even though what is understood will change as our vision becomes broader and our understanding deepens.

What this tells me is that even when I feel pretty certain about something, what I think I know is actually incomplete. There is always more.

It's a lot like climbing up a mountain. The higher you go, the farther you can see. Perhaps that is why Dr. Hawkins says it is much safer to qualify our strong beliefs by saying something like, "Or so it seems to me at the present moment."

Sounds like a good idea to me.

Week 145. Becoming the River

We have spoken a number of times about letting go and letting the river take us where it will, but what if you didn't just go with the river? What if you became the river? What if its current was your heartbeat? What if you opened your heart so much that the river's movement became your movement? And the river's intention was your desire? What if you let go so completely that you were like a wave on the river, in perfect harmony with the forces at work in your life? What would that be like?

Certainly that would be different. There wouldn't be any need to control, only the desire to align. No need to criticize or condemn, for there would only be love. Even intentions and desires would be transformed into simply being free. Being whole. Being the love and the joy that continually want to pour out through your open heart.

When I was a child, I clearly remember running through the grass at twilight, spinning, twirling, falling down, getting up, just letting my feet take me where they would. "I" wasn't really doing it. The joy of the moment was simply moving through me.

Life can be a lot like that when we are willing to let go and let our days unfold according to a plan and a wisdom we cannot see. That wisdom is always working toward our highest good.

When we can do that, we aren't just "going with the flow." We are the flow.

Week 146. How We See Others

How we live our lives says a lot about who or what we think we are, but has it ever occurred to you that how we live our lives says a lot about who or what we think others are, too? Just stop and think about it. Even the clerk in the store. The kid going down the street. The beggar on the corner. The salesman at the door. The person who keeps calling to sell you what you don't want. No matter who it is, how we "see" them in our heart will have a direct effect on how they see themselves.

No matter who we encounter, let's be asking ourselves what is the very best we can see in someone, and then respond accordingly.

Week 147. A Good Answer

Have you ever been in a situation where you just didn't know what to say or do? I know I have. Many times. When some kind of response is needed, what to do then?

Perhaps at times like that, words aren't really necessary. Perhaps just a gentle hand on the shoulder, or a hug, or a nod of the head would do.

I heard a long time ago that silence is often the best answer. Then how can we best respond without saying something? Well, here's a thought—how about a smile, or a chuckle, or a laugh? Laughing breaks up tension and brings things back to a more even keel.

I wish I knew who said a good laugh is worth a thousand right answers, because he was right.

Week 148. Honoring Your Gifts

Have you ever longed to do something you've never done before, something that calls to you from your deepest heart? Perhaps there is a talent you'd like to explore, or a skill that you've never given yourself permission to develop. Those calls—those longings—are there for a reason. If we don't follow our heart's calling, we will never know the joy of fulfilling our potential.

It can take courage and faith, perseverance and determination, to walk into the unknown. Yet if we don't at least try, we will never know what might have been possible.

In his book, *Eternal Echoes, Celtic Reflections on Our Yearning to Belong*, John O'Donohue says our gifts aren't given to us just for our own private use. He says our gifts are given to be shared. The joy you find in following your heart's leading is its gift to you.

There you have it. Our gifts are given to us for a reason. What you do with them is your gift to all whom your life touches.

Week 149. The Prodigal Son

Sometimes we have to feel about as lost as we can be before we are ready to change the direction we are going. This truth is reflected perfectly in the parable of the prodigal son. Once he was willing to face the results of his choices, he knew he had to change his ways and "return home."

He did not know he would be welcomed with open arms. He had not yet realized that he was loved and accepted so completely that there was nothing to forgive.

God's love is like that. Even though we are still in the process of becoming, all the while—through thick and thin, through mistakes and whatever else we do—God sees us only as His beloved children.

No matter where we are in life, we can always turn toward the Lord. We can always decide to change what we are doing and do as the prodigal son did by "going home." When we do, we find the love, acceptance and the guidance that have always been there, just waiting for us.

Week 150. That Underlying, Unalterable Truth

From time immemorial, people have been asking, "What is that underlying, unalterable truth that never changes?"

The human mind cannot fully grasp what that highest truth is, but we can aspire toward it. We can let the highest truth we can understand be the measuring stick for how we live our lives.

This is important—perhaps even more important than we realize. When we seek to align ourselves with the highest truth as we see it, our lives become more sane. We are more in sync with the Love that is seeking to express Itself through us. Yes, and life begins to flow for us.

The ancient sages said over and over, "Truth alone prevails." They were right, of course.

Week 151. Nothing Is Lacking

Whenever we find ourselves asking for something when we pray, Author Mark Nepo says we should stop and start over. He says we should do that as many times as necessary until we can finally be still enough to listen. When we listen deeply, intently, we open to what we sense but cannot hear in our own inner depths where eternal tides are born. If we do this often enough, we begin creating what Nepo calls still points that help us live more peacefully in the world.

Meditation is never about getting something, nor is it about doing something. It is simply about being still, being open, being aware.

When you can do that, the questions just fall away. They would have to, because nothing is lacking. What you already are is more than enough.

Week 152. Listening to Your Body

We all have a built-in internal guidance system, and it is faultless in its direction. That system is our bodymind, and it speaks to us clearly with signals of comfort or discomfort. If your body is comfortable about something, then you're probably on the right track. However, if your body is not comfortable about something, by all means listen to that message. There is a reason for that feeling. Author Tom Robbins calls those signals "yuk" and "yum," a pretty apt description of what your body is trying to say.

Yes, there were times when I've overridden my body's signals and did something anyway. Just so you know, there is always a price to pay when you don't listen to what your body is saying, but that's another story for another time.

Suffice it to say, listen to what your body is telling you. Practice with small things. Which can of beans should I buy? Which street should I turn down? Learn to listen, to really hear, what your body is telling you.

The more you do it, the easier it gets. Then, when the really big decisions come, you will have developed a level of trust with that inner connection. You'll know at a very deep level that what your body says is best for you.

A doctor told me a long time ago, "Listen to your body! It never lies!" Whether or not that happens is up to you. It's one of the most important choices you can make.

Week 153. Light's Lesson

In *Seven Thousand Ways to Listen*, Author Mark Nepo talks about how young trees reach for the light with their branches. As they get older, some of the branches start falling off until eventually the ones that are left are free to just stand in the light.

As I was reading this, I couldn't help thinking what a wonderful metaphor that is for us! We spend most of our lives reaching for the light, never realizing that the light is already within us, right where we are. Obviously, if the light is already in you, you don't need to reach for it. You are the light and the light is you.

All that remains is to just be.

Week 154. Feeling Hurt

Years ago, someone hurt me so deeply I didn't know how to respond. All I could do was take it into the silence and ask for help. That's what I did for the rest of the afternoon.

After a while, it occurred to me that I was fortunate to be the do-ee and not the do-er. This realization made it possible for me to feel compassion for the other person instead of anger and hurt. Now, whenever I think of her, I send thoughts of gratitude. If she hadn't done what she did, I would not have learned such an important lesson.

You see, whenever you want to change a situation, that change has to happen within yourself. It is up to you to restore your own harmony and balance. The amazing thing is, when you do find your own inner peace, everything else comes back into balance as well.

Week 155. The Hottest Fire

Several years ago, when someone was talking about how difficult life had become, our beloved Roger Gabriel responded, "The finest yield is through the hottest fire."

No doubt we can all relate to what he is saying. If we can, then we also understand why he says that nothing in life is ever wasted.

When the going gets tough, just remember you are working on something. Whatever it is, it's probably important.

Week 156. Never Say Never!

Sixty years ago my children gave me a "Chinese Evergreen." It was modest in size, but healthy. The plant grew and grew. Eventually, long gangly "arms" reached way out over the edges of its pot until they nearly caused the plant to topple over from their weight. Several times, out of sheer compassion, I've cut those long arms back to save it from itself. No matter. It continued to grow—until it bloomed!

I didn't know this species could bloom, yet mine did when it was fifty-six years old! I was amazed. Every year since then it has produced more blossoms than the year before.

Then last week, when I was walking through the meditation room, I stopped in my tracks. I couldn't believe my eyes. It was getting ready to bloom again! In January! And it is 60 years old!

Now, whenever I walk by, it seems like I can hear it whispering, "Never say never!"

Message received! Thank you, my long-time green and growing friend.

Year Four

Week 157. New Beginnings

Traditionally, the beginning of a new year is when we try to make a fresh start, to change old habits, to set out on a new path.

When you stop and think about it, every day can be a new start. This day has never happened before. We can do things differently. We can change directions. We can let go of the past and let this day be all it can be.

Yes, and we can enjoy life! We can give thanks! We can count our blessings! We can say "Yes!" to whatever we want and "No" to all of the rest.

Each day is special in itself. Make it what you want it to be so you can look back on it and recognize it for the gift that it truly is.

Week 158. A Work of the Soul

Did you know our darkest, most difficult moments have the greatest potential for positive growth? They grab our attention and don't let go until we have worked our way through to the other side. They even teach us to turn to a "higher power" for help.

Working through challenge is always a work of the soul. The wisdom and strength we need can only come through our soul. Many times we live our lives not giving any thought to our soul. This is unfortunate. It is when we connect with our Source in the depths of our soul that we find our way back into the light.

Week 159. Gratitude

There is a precious story about an old coal miner who sat down to his evening meal of thin soup and a piece of bread. His hands were dirty from the mines, his hair unkempt, but his heart was full as he looked at his meal and said, "All this, and Jesus, too!"

This story makes me think about how grateful we can be when we look back at where our lives have gone and where we are now. Truly, challenges and all, our cup does run over. We are so blessed.

When life gets hectic and the hours are full, let's remember to meet each day with gratitude.

Week 160. Listening to Your Heart

Sometimes we start off in one direction and end up going in another. Perhaps it was intuition that took us in an unexpected direction. Or maybe it was our heart that spoke to us.

Either way, we all have an inner voice we sense but cannot hear. This is the part of us that knows. If we would follow it, we must trust in what we are hearing.

Sometimes the only way we can know if we've taken the right path is by having the courage to follow where our heart is leading us. That is just one reason why going into the silence is so important. When we tap into the part of us that knows, we bypass all the "shoulds" and "oughts" that confuse the issue and constrict our freedom to choose.

We may not always know if we made the "right" choice, at least not right away. Yet this much is certain—if we are ever to grow inwardly, we must be willing to explore the unknown.

Week 161. We Are Always Whole

When we learn to trust the Hand that is always guiding us, we find both meaning and purpose in the challenges we are facing.

As unwelcome as adversity may be, it does shape and define us in ways that nothing else can. With time, we learn to let go and accept what we cannot change. Acceptance is the beginning of our healing. It allows us to use our pain as a means of growth. It helps enormously if we can reconnect with our Creator's quiet, loving presence. If we do that often enough, that Presence becomes a haven for us, a place we can always return to for rest and renewal.

Eventually, we begin to understand that our thoughts, our life, and even our death are just stages in our journey.

Week 162. Obstacles or Opportunities?

There have been times in my life when I was trying to move in a certain direction and things kept getting in the way. Perhaps you've had this happen, too. It never occurred to me that those things were there for a reason, so I just kept on struggling against what was in my way. It wasn't until many years later that I learned to stop resisting what was happening and just go with the flow.

Accepting "what is" requires practice. Resistance, on the other hand, is like trying to swim upstream. Life gives us endless opportunities to practice what we need to learn. When we're on the "right" path, there are no obstacles, only opportunities. Opportunities to practice. Opportunities to grow.

I think Mary O'Malley must have known this when she said: "What's in the way is the way." She was right, of course.

Week 163. Holy Ground

A stem of exquisite white frilly iris is in a bud vase on my dining table, and it has changed my day completely. It has three buds on it. One bud is fat and full and no doubt will soon begin opening. One is starting to open. As I watch it, I can feel its excitement, even its wonder, over what is happening to it. The joy it is feeling is palpable, at least it is to me. The third blossom is in full bloom and is amazing to behold. Its wide open petals speak not only of its joy but of the wonder of surrender and awe that so much beauty could come through it.

This single iris stem says so much about you and me. We, too, have potential within us that we haven't yet begun to imagine. As that potential does begin to blossom, we are filled with wonder that something that special could be coming through us.

When our spirit is in bloom, when we are fully open to That which is within us, we move beyond all language. All we can do is bask in the magnificence of the inner splendor we are discovering.

I am reminded of the story in the Bible where Moses was told to take off his shoes because he was standing on holy ground. (Exodus 3:5)

Today my kitchen has become a sanctuary. It has become holy ground. How do I know? The iris told me.

Week 164. Making a Difference

There are so many remarkable people who have come and gone in this world. Even though we may not have heard about them, they made a great difference in the lives of others. One such person was Peter Milne. Peter was a Presbyterian minister who began serving in the New Hebrides Islands in 1870. He was what people called a "one-way missionary" because he chose to serve in an area where missionaries were routinely killed on arrival. That did not stop Peter. He felt called to go there and he served the local tribes for 35 years until his passing.

While there, Peter translated the Bible and other religious books into the local language of Efatese. Just as important, perhaps even more so, was how he served the people there with an open, loving heart. When he died (of natural causes), the people buried him in the middle of the town and put the following inscription on his tombstone: "When he came, there was no light. When he died, there was no darkness."

We all make a difference, each in our own way. The most significant difference we make is usually done unconsciously by just being what we are. How we live our lives is silent testimony to the truths we harken to.

Let's all ask ourselves how we are honoring the truths we truly believe. As surely as night follows day, whatever is coloring our life is affecting the lives of others, too.

Week 165. Being the Change

One of the examples I like to use when I teach our meditation course is how a drop of ink changes the color of all the water. Obviously, I'm not the first person who thought of this. What makes this concept so special is that every time you have a kind thought, or do a kind deed, everyone benefits. More than that, every time you meditate, it raises the level of human consciousness just that much more.

You see, you never do anything just for yourself, even though it may seem so at the time. In changing yourself, in aligning yourself with what is good and true and beautiful, you change your world. You may not see the change right away, but it is there, and it is cumulative.

If you are wondering what one person can possibly do to alleviate the turmoil in today's world, simply be the change you want to see. (Thank you, Gandhi.)

It does make a difference. More than you know.

Week 166. Thank Your Body

When I was doing my early morning stretches today, I got to thinking about what a finely tuned instrument the body is, how it responds to absolutely every thought and feeling we have. I find that pretty amazing.

With a gift like that, it only seems natural to be grateful for this body we have been given, but have you ever thought about thanking your body for all it does for you? When I first heard that idea, it seemed a bit far out to say that every living system is responsive to your thoughts and feelings and the energy you just naturally radiate.

If this is so, then your body is no exception, so yes, do talk to your body. Thank it for its faithfulness, for its efficiency, for how well it serves you. Make sure it gets the rest, nourishment, and exercise it needs. How well you take care of your body determines how well it can serve you. As my husband used to say, "You have to take care of the old equipment if you want the old equipment to take care of you." He was right.

Week 167. The Inner Call

The Sufi poet, Rumi, says we should be grateful for whatever it is that calls us to return to our center. Why? Because it very well could be an invitation from the Lord.

Too often we get lost in all the outer distractions. Even when we do, that longing, that hidden truth is still there. It's lurking around the edges, hiding in the wind, dancing around us, hoping to capture our attention. That nudging is a call from within, one we seldom listen to until we have reason to, but the call is always there. If we heed that call, if we follow its leading, sooner or later we'll hear its mystical song echoing in our deepest heart of hearts and we'll know that while we may not be there yet, we are on our way home.

Our spiritual journey is like that. Even when we do not know where we're going, or why, there is a certainty we cannot shake that we are on a trail that will lead us to what we have forgotten. As we follow that trail, we may find it necessary to embrace a larger way of being if we want to embrace a greater purpose in life.

That larger way of being is, in fact, our destiny. It is what we have been searching for all along.

Week 168. A Rather Radical Suggestion

Everywhere I go, I feel the undercurrent speeding up. People are trying to do more and do it faster. The newspapers, TV, even the mail all encourage us to move at a faster pace that goes with doing and wanting more, more, more.

Today I'm going to make what may seem like a rather radical suggestion. I'm going to suggest that we all set a deliberate intention to slow down. Let's move through life with an eye more on the quality of our days instead of how much we can cram into them. In many ways, less really is more: less chaos—more peace, less stress—more joy, less busy-ness—more time to be with those we love and care about.

Wouldn't it be wonderful if we could experience each day as the gift it truly is? If we could find those deeper moments that bring special meaning and joy to our spirit?

No doubt there are many ways to do that. One way which particularly speaks to me is to simply go with what warms your heart. Listen to your heart and honor what your heart is saying. Your heart is never wrong.

Every day is precious. What better way to honor the sanctity of this moment—this day—this life—than paying attention to where your heart is leading you?

Week 169. How We See Others

Author and Speaker Jean Houston says we empower each other when we recognize our hidden potential. This is one of the greatest gifts we can offer.

Her statement got me to wondering how often we focus on the greatness in each other. Instead we live our lives judging each other. We've forgotten that judgment is always relative, rarely based on the deeper truths that lie hidden within us.

What would our days be like if we actually spent some time thinking about the people in our lives and seeing them at the highest and best we can possibly imagine? If you've ever done this, you already know how that changes your perception. You see them differently. How you feel about them changes, too.

There is a rather odd twist to this exercise, because when you see others in their highest light, how you feel about yourself gets elevated, too.

A particularly good place to begin this practice is with a difficult relationship. Is there someone you aren't quite seeing eye to eye with, someone who "gets under your skin," who makes life less than easy for you? If so, then start there, and see what happens.

As my very dear friend, Libby, often says, "I will if you will. I mean what's the best that could happen?"

Week 170. Laws

According to the Yurok Indians, being true to yourself means doing your best to help a person in need. Not only that, being true to yourself is the one and only Yurok Indian law.

What a powerful premise! Here we are with all of these laws, when all we need to do is be true to ourself! I think most of us already know that, but how often do we think about it? How often do we do it?

When I came across this statement, it got me wondering about the laws that are governing our lives. I'm not talking about legislated laws. I'm talking about the precepts we hold as our standard for living.

Let's all think about that, and see what we find.

Week 171. Looking Behind the Curtain

There have been many times in my life when I have wondered what possible good could come from some particular situation. If we were to look "behind the curtain," as Deepak would say, we might see that these very situations offer us the opportunity to learn more about who we are and why we are here. Learning to accept and work through our challenges is how life helps us grow and mature. Struggle leads us to our own inner wisdom.

While it can be helpful to look to others for confirmation, the light we seek is always within us. As we learn to align ourselves with the Higher Will and attune our inner ear to its whisper, we will be guided in just the right way, at just the right time. All we have to do is stop and listen.

A good way to jump start the process is by paying attention to your body. What is it telling you? Is it comfortable about what you are considering, or not? There is this much about it—your body always knows what is best.

The next time you aren't sure about something, listen to your body. Then follow what it tells you. You'll be glad that you did.

Week 172. It's About Love

I've often wondered why certain things have come into my life. Perhaps you have, too. Over time, I've come to understand that the reason was love. It may not have seemed like it at the time. Yet at the core, where the real meaning lies, it was all about love.

I can't explain that. I won't even try, but it's true. Once you know that, it gets a lot easier to go with what is—whatever it is—because then you know that love is at work in your life and that all is well, whether it seems like it or not.

The other day I was looking at the back of a piece of very fine needlework. What I saw was a lot of knots and loose threads. Not much of it made any sense, but when I turned it over, what I saw was so beautiful it brought tears to my eyes.

Life is a lot like that. While we may not understand the knots and loose threads in our lives, if we peek through the veil that dims our vision, we would see—we would feel—the infinite love that is behind all of it.

We can't always see beyond that veil, but we can tune into the love. We can look for its presence in everything. Yes, and we can be that love, no matter what. We can let that love translate itself into what we do and what we are.

When that happens, you'll know for yourself that love is all there is—and you are that love.

Week 173. Walking

There are so many ways to walk, and each of them reflects a state of mind. One of my favorite ways to walk is early in the morning as the sun is rising. It's a time to gather my thoughts, my energy, and myself together. When I'm walking outside, the dew-covered grass reminds me of the manna that fell so many years ago for the Israelites. It reminds me of how our needs are always supplied, how we are always watched over and cared for.

There are other ways to walk, too. Hurriedly down a hospital corridor. Anxious steps. Thoughtful steps. Steps filled with prayer. Steps filled with hope.

The other end of the spectrum would be happy steps. Bubbly steps. I love to watch the way my great granddaughter, Bella, walks. She giggles when she does it. The joy of life just spills out of her. What a good reminder that this same joy is in me, too. If I just pay attention, I will find it.

Even the seasons have their influence on how we walk. November finds me taking grateful steps as I get together with friends, or walk into the grocery store, or when I go into my office to wrap gifts and prepare to send notes to family and friends. I'm grateful for the love and memories we share.

Perhaps the most important way to walk would be walking with the Lord, mindful of how His Presence is always with us and within us. When we are feeling up or when we are feeling down, that Presence is always here, always working to make the going easier.

Life is a partnership with our Creator. If we can just remember that, then surely we will be able to walk in peace and gratitude each and every day.

Week 174. Moving Beyond Our Limitations

When I was re-reading Richard Bach's book, *Illusions*, I came across the following lines: "Argue for your limitations, and sure enough, they're yours."

His words got me to thinking about all of the things I've believed that seemed so true when they were really just my point of view.

Deepak says our perception shapes our reality. Experience tells me it is also true that when we change our perception, our reality changes, too.

Quite some time ago, I heard that the answer to a problem is never at the level of the problem. We have to rise above the problem—transcend would be a good word—to find the solution. A broader perspective does do wonders.

Let's all take a good honest look at the beliefs we entertain. If you find some attitudes you wish weren't so, see if you can find a thought that is a little closer to how you'd like things to be.

Esther Hicks talked about this when I heard her in California. She said you don't go from anger to bliss in one small step. It takes a lot of small steps that move in the direction of bliss to get you there. She was right.

Whatever it is you come up with that you'd like to change, if you can't find the whole answer right now, see if you can find part of it. Even small steps are an indication of progress.

As I said many times on the golf course (particularly after having hit a rather poor shot), forward is progress. Indeed it is.

Week 175. The Ebb and Flow of Life

When I read Swami Rama's statement that we should use our harshest sorrows, as well as our greatest joys, for growth and wisdom, I was deep in my harshest sorrow.

Making full use of every experience was a totally new concept for me. I'd always thought we just had to find a way to get through our difficulties. Trying to make use of them opened an entirely new way of seeing things.

As I tried to apply his advice, I soon learned that it isn't what happens to you but how you use it to further your growth that makes a difference. You don't have to just lie down and let the train run over you. You can seek out the lessons, the wisdom, even the gift that often comes in the form of growth as you mount your challenge and ride it through to the other side.

Swami's words came straight to the front of my mind again this week when I woke up to find my basement had flooded after six inches of rain overnight. It isn't easy to look for the "rainbow" when you're in the midst of a mess like that. However, if one tries, the insights that present themselves can be truly surprising. One of those insights became my "daytime mantra" as we moved furniture, pulled up carpet, threw out padding, etc, etc, etc. The mantra was: "It's only water." Repeating those three words over and over helped create a brighter perspective as we worked through all that had to be done.

There is an ebb and flow to life. Some periods are smooth, others are not. The next time you find yourself encountering "rough weather," I hope Swami Rama's counsel will inspire you to find a way to rise above the challenge and find the wisdom that is hidden in it.

Week 176. Living from Within

Erich Schiffmann says meditating isn't just about quieting the mind. It's about tuning in. It's about connecting with your inner stillness and resting it. He's talking about listening to your own inner guidance system, and then following that wisdom.

Meditation and yoga and their related practices are actually tools that can help you develop a relationship with your own Infinite Spirit. That is what "yoga" means—union. When you begin to feel that connection, life takes on new meaning for you.

When you pay attention inwardly, a deep sense of knowing develops within you. You know because you are tuned in to the subtle promptings that only your spirit can recognize. It takes a lot of courage, especially at first, to follow leadings you can't explain. The more you do it, the more you learn to trust them until eventually, living from within becomes a way of life.

Week 177. Food for Thought

Shams of Tabriz, who was Rumi's immortal companion, said we should learn to love life and all that life brings. That can be a pretty tall assignment when the changes we are confronted with are those we instinctively resist, but Shams knew a secret. He knew that resistance would just add to the difficulty of the situation. Instead, he suggested just letting life live itself through you. He said not to worry if your life is turning upside down. After all, how do you know that what you are used to is better than what is to come?

Food for thought—wouldn't you say?

Week 178. Making Inner Changes

Gandhi believed that everyone has seeds of greatness. If he was going to grow into his highest and best, he knew he was going to have to practice the principles he wanted to build his life around. He had to live his truth before he could be it. That was going to mean a lot of inner work because Gandhi was a misfit, but that didn't stop him. Once he committed to changing himself, he never wavered. He did whatever it took to shed the personal qualities that stood in his way.

Gandhi believed his calling would find him, so he simply surrendered to the Higher Will and let that Will shape him. After Gandhi had grown into his calling, people would tell him that his example was too difficult for them to follow. Either they didn't understand the principle behind it, or it required too much change for them to embrace it. His reply was to commit to what they did know to be true, and build on that.

That principle is one we all can follow. If we commit to what we know to be true, the rest will take care of itself.

Week 179. Exploring

When you stop and think about it, we're a lot like explorers, finding our way through the maze of life, climbing unknown mountains, taking untried routes, trying to get wherever our heart wants to take us. Sometimes the journey is easy, even fun. At other times, the road becomes difficult, but not to despair. Eternal forces are always supporting us and helping us achieve our deepest desires.

Sometimes the only way we can get where we want to go is to learn what we need to learn so that door can open. This is true whatever we are working on. There is this much about it—when you are true to your inner leading, the support will be there. As Deepak has often said, "When you go where your dharma leads, you are following a thread that will never break."

Week 180. Opening to the Infinite

Even in the midst of seeming chaos, harmony and order are intact. If we can learn to look beyond what is apparent to what is eternal, we discover that we are both the flow and we are the stream.

We connect with our own inner stillness when we go beyond our mind to our ground state of Pure Being. At that deep level there is no thought at all, yet there is an unshakable knowingness that comes just from having been there. That core knowledge is what allowed the ancient sages to say, "I am That, you are That, all this is That, and That's all there is."

They were right, of course.

Week 181. Patience

If you're like me, there are times when I want something to happen and I want it to happen now. I don't want to wait. I want to get it behind me. I want it to be done and over with so I can move on to something else. Whenever I feel this way, it doesn't happen, and I do have to wait. Gratefully, I am learning that when those times come, the best thing I can do is surrender to the process. I need to accept that I'm really not in control, nor was I ever in control.

That's what we humans want, isn't it—to be in control? However, if we stopped and thought about it, there is a deeper issue here. That issue has to do with being aligned with the Higher Will. When that is what we truly want, then God's timing isn't a problem. We know that whatever is for our highest good will come at just the right time, in just the right way.

In other words, what we really need to do is trust—in God's timing, and in the Higher Wisdom that is always at work in our lives.

Week 182. Grudges

Many years ago I was complaining to a dear friend. Her response? "Donna, don't hug a thistle!" I'd not heard that before, nor had I thought about it in quite that way, but that is exactly what I was doing. When we hang on to perceived hurts, those "grudges" can get so deeply embedded in our consciousness that their energy colors everything we do. No wonder we don't have peace in our world when we can't even have peace in our heart!

According to Eknath Easwaran, there were ancient sages who actually didn't understand what resentment was. Their hearts were so full of love, there was nothing to forgive, nothing to resent, even nothing over which to become angry!

Let's all see if we can fill our days with a love like that. If we do, peace will automatically become part of the fabric of our lives.

Week 183. Real Honor

Badshah Kahn, who became a great friend and supporter of Gandhi, was a visionary and leader of the Pathan people who lived where the borders of India and Pakistan meet. Those tribes have been lost in history, yet their story—and Badshah's story—hold clues that could change the course of today's history if we could just hear their message. You see, the Pathans built their lives around a code of honor that required revenge and violence. Badshah knew that his courageous people were bound by ancient custom, so he dedicated himself to freeing them by educating and inspiring them to live by a higher code of ethics. He believed if they could find a new form of honor, they would turn away from their tradition of violence. He was right.

What did he do? Badshah taught his beloved Pathans that love is far more powerful than bombs, that kindness is true strength, and the only way to be truly brave is to be in the right. Because of his example, thousands upon thousands of his people sacrificed their lives as they worked along with Khan and Gandhi to nonviolently free both India and Pakistan from British rule.

The strength that came through their belief in nonviolence allowed these brave people to re-define what honor meant. Not only did it change their lives, it changed the world.

That being so, it seems appropriate to stop and ask ourselves what honor means to us, because whatever honor means to each one of us most surely is shaping our world.

Week 184. Sacred Encounters

There is something pure and fresh about new snow. Everything seems to take on a touch of holiness as the marks of civilization are swept away in that pristine beauty. At such moments, you can feel the silence, and you know that at some deep level you, too, are timeless, untouched, and whole. Somehow you sense that what is being you is being the cosmos, too. You feel connected to Something larger, Something of which you are a part.

Such sacred encounters are the soul's response to solitude. They cannot be bought. They can only be given. That happens when we surrender to That which is seeking to express Itself through us, too. For just a moment we glimpse the deeper place our soul knows as home. The nostalgia we feel is a sign of our silent recognition.

Somehow, somewhere, we know we are more—far more—than the chaos around us. To tap into that "something more" is to find strength for the journey. It is to know you are not alone. It is to taste the mystery that can only be found in the silence that is here now, quietly waiting for us. It only asks for our attention.

Week 185. When Silence Calls

I'd gone to the mountains to attend a meeting, but that first night I gave myself the evening. I had to. I had not slept. My body was weary, but my soul said, "Write," so write I did, and then I walked.

The air was sweet and fragrant, the hills filled with color, and in the distance I could see where it was raining on nearby mountains. There were occasional streaks of lightning, while far away the sun was setting. God is truly the master artist. I stood there and let the magnificence fill my soul. I was in a special space, very much in touch with my deeper layers, and I was grateful.

When I'm in a space like that, it is easy to write, so I thought, and I walked, and then I wrote some more. I could tell my soul was asking for attention. "I have something I want to tell you," it seemed to be saying. "Will you listen?"

Yes, I will listen—and gladly, for never have I been sorry when my soul wanted to speak. Always the words have been like rain on parched land, like moonlight and starlight on a cloudless night. Insights it brought me. A new way of seeing things. A clearer view of my hidden depths. For just a moment, the curtain parted, and there was That which I'd been seeking. Better than glitter and gold by far, such moments make a king's riches seem poor and paltry at best.

What we're talking about is intimacy—intimacy with ourself, intimacy with our soul. Who is to say if they are different? For many of us, that kind of intimacy is like a foreign land. We've heard about it, but we've never been there.

It seems strange that we seek intimacy with others, but never with ourself. What is at the root of our hesitancy? True, many of us were taught not to be selfish, but being selfish is not the same as knowing—and caring—about yourself.

Someone told me long ago that you have to be self-ish before you can be selfless. I've found that to be true. We must nurture ourself if we would give out of our fullness rather than our dregs.

There are so many ways to nurture yourself. We each must find the way best suited to us. Always we must choose. There are voices all around us, and within us as well. To whom shall we listen? To whom shall we give the gift of our attention? For me it must be my soul. Ever and always, when the silence calls, may I be its faithful audience. May I leave all my humble treasures at its feet for the singular joy of being in its presence.

Week 186. Finding the Silence

Frequently, I hear people say the thoughts they have during their meditation prevent them from reaching the silence. While that may be true, what we've forgotten is that we are the silence, and that silent inner state is always aware.

That awareness is always here because we are always here. If you're having trouble "finding the silence," what you're really saying is you've lost touch with your own inner being.

Here's a suggestion—start by looking for the silence even when you aren't meditating! Just notice those moments where all is quiet and nothing is happening. Once you can do that, turn your attention to who is doing the noticing. In fact, right now, right where you are, just look around you. No labeling. No judging, only noticing. Do you feel a sense of presence? Well, that presence—that awareness—is you!

The next time moments of quiet slip into your life, see if you can be aware of how infinite that stillness is, how it resonates deep within you. That deep sense of awareness is your soul. The more attuned you are to this ever-present silent state and its infinite wisdom, the better you'll be able to ride the deeper currents of your life.

Week 187. Embracing Solitude

Even though Gladys Taber's book, *Another Path*, has been around for quite a while, I never tire of reading it. You see, Gladys found a way to make peace with being alone, and she did that by opening herself to the beauty all around her. Embracing the silence and the peace she found in Nature opened her to that same spaciousness in herself. She began to feel connected to a larger way of being. Of course, to do that she had to step out of the frantic pace that had consumed her life for so long. It was a fruitful choice that taught her much. "Fog is not forever," she tells us, "nor is night a permanent condition." I think we all have times when we need to be reminded of that.

Gladys' message makes me wonder why we don't spend more time nurturing our deep levels, too. You might want to ask yourself when you last gave yourself a chance to stop and just be for a little while. If you haven't done that recently, then how about making an appointment with yourself to go find a wooded spot, a lake or a stream, or just sit quietly and watch the sun set? Times such as these expand your spirit and feed your soul.

Life is full of wonder. That wonder can be yours when you stop and pay attention. Perhaps your soul is calling to you even now. Will you stop and listen? If not now, when?

Week 188. A Higher Plan

It is easy to get discouraged when life gets tough and struggles overwhelm us. When those times come, and they do for all of us, it is important to remember that "even this" is part of our inner growth. Nothing is wasted.

A favorite hymn from my childhood speaks of "my gold to refine and my dross to consume." That is what the fire of challenge does. It pushes our growing edge and creates a hunger that only spiritual growth can satisfy. It helps—a lot—if we can trust that God is working His purpose out in ways we may not understand but which serve a very real purpose in our lives. When we align our sails with that Higher Plan, we begin moving in sync with the Hand that is seeking to guide us.

Aurobindo, that great sage from the 20th Century, encourages us to align our intentions and desires with that greater Wisdom. According to him, when we choose to align with the Infinite, the end for which we silently hunger is assured.

We are never lost, no matter how tough the road gets. There is a purpose at work in our lives, whether we can see it or not.

Isn't that all we really need to know?

Week 189. When Life Becomes Magical

Life is constantly mirroring our inner state back to us in the hope that we can begin to understand how we are creating our world. The key is learning to recognize this silent signal. We are so accustomed to judging our experiences when what we really need to do is accept that what we are seeing is our own attitude being mirrored back to us.

Judging things as good or bad brings the polarities into play. If we can detach from the need to judge, then our lives, our bodies and our experiences will open to the peace, the clarity and the vitality that are our natural state.

Life is always seeking to move us in the direction of peace and joy. Once we open our heart and walk in sync with that inner leading, life becomes magical.

Week 190. Meister Eckhart

Meister Eckhart was way ahead of his time. So far ahead, in fact, that he was widely criticized for his outrageous thinking. While humanity as a whole may have made some progress spiritually since those medieval times, his thinking is still considered above the curve.

For example, he says we limit God when we ask for something specific. Eckhart must have known we are on the wrong track when we look for our fulfillment in the things of this world. God's Wisdom and Love are more than enough to fill all of our hopes and dreams.

In fact, he suggests that we just seek God, and forget about the rest. After all, if you don't have a relationship with God, you'll never be satisfied anyway.

Week 191. A Great Liberation

Deepak says everyone is doing the best they can at any given moment. That thought was a great liberation for me. As I thought about it, I realized I was always doing the best I could, regardless of the mistakes I felt I'd made. I finally understood that mistakes just show us where there is room to grow. That's where compassion comes in.

It's one thing to feel compassion for others, it's quite another to have compassion for yourself. If you don't have compassion for yourself, you can't really feel compassion toward someone else, can you?

Bottom line? Forget about being perfect! You're already perfect, just the way you are. The reason you don't see this is because you're still growing. That growth is part of your perfection.

I like how Leonard Cohen says it—"Everything has a crack in it. That's how the light gets in."

Week 192. When It's Raining

I was up at the farm this past weekend visiting my daughter and son-in-law and their family. While I was there, I happened to see this on their wall:

"Life isn't about waiting for the storm to pass. It's about learning to dance in the rain."

That pretty much says it all, doesn't it?

Week 193. Unseen Currents

If you've ever spent any time at the beach, as I did recently, then no doubt you've watched the shore birds gliding on unseen currents of air. It was a mesmerizing sight, and it got me to wondering about the unseen currents at work in our lives.

Just what are those invisible forces and influences? Where do you suppose they came from? Are we able to trust them just as freely and completely as these feathered creatures do? Somehow those birds are able to put their whole trust in that which is supporting them even though they cannot see what it is. Perhaps instinct teaches them to do that, but don't we have an instinct, too? Isn't there an unseen support at work in our lives that we can depend on just as completely?

If you can trust those deep inner currents that are ever seeking to guide you, then surely you will be able to move through difficult times confident in the knowledge that love is at work in your life, regardless of the form it takes.

Week 194. Nature Speaks

This past week I had the privilege of standing at the base of Multnomah Falls just outside of Portland, Oregon. The Falls are so high, you have to strain your neck to see the top. This time of year, the Falls were lacy and sheer. It was a mesmerizing sight to watch that unending stream of free-falling water as it cascaded down the mountainside in ever-changing patterns until it reached the pool below. It was one of those timeless moments that touched upon the feeling of eternity.

I couldn't help thinking about what it would be like if we could let go just as completely to the Higher Will. Who knows what we might become if we could surrender to the destiny that awaits us as we move through our own evolution. I say that because there is a Presence and a Power that are waiting to release within us what has been hidden for ages and generations.

Once we can see beyond who we think we are, we will discover the vastness within us that has been waiting for our attention.

If you haven't been out in Nature lately, I encourage you to do so. In her own silent way, Nature whispers truths we cannot hear any other way. All we have to do is listen.

Week 195. Forces of the Universe

Three forces that are always at work in the universe are creation, maintenance, and dissolution. Most of us are pretty comfortable with the first two. In fact, we spend quite a bit of time and energy trying to maintain our health, finances, relationships, etc. It's the third one that we're not as willing to accept as a normal part of life, but without dissolution, the entire formula would break down.

Dr. Hawkins says every stage is perfect in itself. An example he sometimes uses is that of a rose. A rosebud is a perfect rosebud, and a rose bloom is a perfect rose bloom. No less perfect is a withered rose. It is perfect in its withered form. Each stage of that unfolding is in perfect sync with the rhythm of the cosmos.

Since we are part of the cosmos, the same is true for your body. While the spirit that inhabits your body is changeless and eternal, your body is subject to these same laws of creation, maintenance, and dissolution. Learning to make peace with the inevitability of those forces is one of the great challenges that comes with being human.

The good news is that there is a part of us that is eternal, that was never born and never dies. When we find that, we've found our way home. As Deepak says, it's a great liberation.

That, of course, is why we meditate.

Week 196. Anger vs Compassion

Someone asked me recently what to do about the anger she was feeling over something that had happened. The answer was simple: "Let go of it!" Easy to say but hard to do? Perhaps, but it does get easier once you recognize that the one you hurt the most when you are angry is yourself.

Even in close relationships, there is much we don't know about the other person. If we did know, we would better understand their behavior. Since we don't, the best we can do is respond with compassion. If they truly knew better, they would do better. If that is the best they honestly feel they can do, then there is ample room for compassion.

While we're at it, let's not forget to offer compassion to ourself, too. We are all doing the best we can at any given moment.

Inside every heart there is a light that is just waiting to shine. Compassion and forgiveness help sweep away the clouds that hide it.

Week 197. Your Inner Solstice

It never ceases to amaze me how a subtle shift of the planet turns the entire Northern Hemisphere toward Spring. Now that the winter solstice is almost here, I'm wondering what simple shift I can make to have my own inner solstice, too. How can I turn my life more toward my deepest desires? Perhaps you are thinking about that, too.

One of the things that goes with this intention is making the time to replenish yourself at a deep level. If this speaks to you, then you might want to ask yourself how you can relax more into your life instead of rushing through it. Alan Watts said it so well. "Life is like music. You don't just play it to get to the end."

How can you make room for what really matters to you? Do you need to create some boundaries that will allow you to do more of what you want to do and not just what you have to do? That might mean having to say "no" sometimes so you can say "yes" to what makes your heart sing.

What does make your heart sing? Only you know the answer to that.

Week 198. How Victories Are Won

Mitch has lived most of his life in a wheelchair. "I don't think of myself as handicapped," he says. "I was born this way, so it doesn't bother me at all." Apparently it doesn't bother his 3-year-old nephew who told him not long ago, "When I grow up, I want to be a wheelchair basketball player, just like you!"

Truly, we are what we think. Life is lived a thought at a time. That's how victories are won. Thought—after thought—after thought.

Week 199. System Restore

My computer has a feature called "System Restore." Perhaps you have that same feature on your computer. As I think about it, that term could apply to more than just computers because your body knows how to restore itself, too. There is a deep wisdom in your body. That wisdom is your own pattern of wholeness. While that pattern can become distorted or clouded or somehow hidden

117

from view, nevertheless it is always there. That is very good news, because that intrinsic wholeness is part of your own nature. It can be forgotten, but it can never be lost.

Is it possible to do a "System Restore" with your body? There are those who say it is. The way you do that is by re-membering or re-minding yourself of what wholeness feels like and what it looks like. Then you set your intention to think thoughts of wholeness and not allow other thoughts to creep in. If you are faithful to your intention, if you hold true to that memory of wholeness, then you have aligned yourself with your body's natural pattern. You are re-minding the body and strengthening its ability to re-store itself. Even though your body knows how to do this, the task becomes much more difficult when you send it thoughts and patterns that do not coincide with its own natural rhythms.

Let's be particularly mindful of the patterns we are sending our body. Dr. Joe Dispenza says it takes a minimum of three weeks of regularly practicing desired thoughts and attitudes to establish them and set them into motion. Let's be steadfast in our resolve. Let's make a commitment to what we want to achieve and give our system the time it takes to set that pattern in motion.

There is a wholeness that goes deeper than this, but since your body is the part of yourself of which you are most aware, let's start there.

Week 200. In God's Economy

In God's economy, nothing is ever wasted. Not ever. All things can—and will—be used for some good purpose. No matter what is going on in your life right now—no matter how good or how difficult —please know that ultimately this, too, will be used for some good purpose.

The how is not up to us. Trusting in the process is.

Week 201. Finding Our Wholeness

Dr. Jon Kabat-Zinn says wholeness and connectedness are part of our fundamental nature. No matter how many emotional scars we carry from the past, our intrinsic wholeness is still intact.

Dr. Jon says it is through meditation that we learn to connect with our underlying wholeness. He also reminds us that we are all part of a larger wholeness that is expressing itself in ways beyond our ability to comprehend. This underlying wholeness is a natural part of us. When we connect with it consciously, we see how that wholeness is being supported by the great stream of consciousness in which we live and move and have our being.

When you truly understand this, then you also know that even in your seeming brokenness, you are still whole. Yes, and that pattern of wholeness will always be within you, regardless of what is happening on the surface.

I hope you find great comfort in that thought. I know I do.

Week 202. Where Forgiving Begins

It's important to remember that the first person you need to forgive is yourself. Until you can love and accept yourself fully and completely, you will not be able to do the same for others.

I've heard it said many times that the person you hurt the most when you harbor negative feelings is yourself. Unfortunately, that simple statement does not tell you how to get rid of those feelings. Isn't that what we really need to know?

Dr. David Simon says we cannot say we have forgiven until we can look in our heart and see only love and compassion. Essentially, what we're talking about is a work of the heart.

The Talmudic sage, Rabbi Eliezer, taught that we should fully make amends for our indiscretions on the day before our death. When his student pointed out that few people can know with certainty that they will die the next day, he replied, "Then, just in case, it might be a good idea to fully atone today."

I hope you're smiling. I know I was when I read that.

119

Week 203. Frustration

It was one of those days when all of the little stuff piled up. I found myself spending a lot of time waiting on the phone while people tried to correct errors that never should have been made. (That's purely my opinion, of course.) At first, I tried to treat it like an exercise, but by the time it got to mid-afternoon, it was finally starting to get to me. Looking for something to do while I sat there "on hold" a-g-a-i-n, I happened to notice a card I'd made some notes on. I picked it up, and here is what I read:

"When you feel yourself getting frustrated, pray, 'Lord, I accept this situation as it is.' Then be still, and without thinking about it, do what must be done with unconditional love and dedication to the truth of your being. Just do what needs to be done in the spirit of selfless service, without attachment to results."

I don't really need to tell you how the rest of my day went after that, do I?

Week 204. Just Being

So much of our life is spent in the fast lane. The momentum just seems to build and build. Meditating provides a gap in your busy-ness and lets you get in touch with yourself.

Ancient scriptures tell us that meditation is a way of getting to know yourself. Rather than trying to achieve perfection, it's more about finding out who and what you really are.

You see, there is an aspect of yourself that is beyond all of your thinking, feeling and doing. Meditating allows you to experience that deeper aspect.

As Deepak would say, there is a big difference between eating a meal and just reading the menu. The same is true with tapping into your inner self. Until you experience it, you simply don't know what being yourself means.

Let's all find time to stop and enjoy the moments of silence life gives us. It's in the silence that you find your answers, your peace, your joy, and yes, yourself.

Week 205. Channeling Grace

As we all know, having the intention to see nobility and beauty in someone is not the same as knowing how to do it, so here are some tips I got from a young man I met in the airport recently who is affiliated with the global Avatar movement. According to Cameron, whether we know someone or not, we can always say in our heart:

Just like me, this person is seeking some happiness in life.

Just like me, this person is trying to avoid suffering.

Just like me, this person has known sadness, loneliness and despair.

Just like me, this person is seeking to fulfill his/her/their needs.

Just like me, this person is learning about life.

That's what we're all doing, isn't it? Every day we're learning something new. While we're learning, we have the chance to bless others simply by recognizing that they have the same needs, the same hopes and fears that we do.

Caroline Myss says we can either offer grace or we can withhold it. That's a pretty tall yardstick, but certainly something we can all aspire to.

Week 206. A Mystery

The other day, I had the opportunity to look through a book of pictures taken by the Hubble telescope. What I saw was mind boggling. There are universes upon universes and even more universes just within our own galaxy, and that's only a tiny part of what the telescope revealed. Beyond our galaxy are billions of other galaxies that seemingly go on forever.

I don't know if you've ever heard of black holes (Deepak is fascinated with them), but if you haven't, it is from black holes that all of this stellar stuff is spewn.

One black hole, the Perseus A, which is 235 million light years across, is a super massive black hole. Ripples in the swirl of gas being sucked into its dark heart reveal the presence of sound waves—a simple, guttural melody: B-flat, 57 octaves beneath middle C and "a million billion times deeper than the limits of human hearing." Yes, the universe is singing! It not only sings, it listens to itself! One of the ways it does that is through you and me!

Beyond the limits of all of these perceivable phenomena is a field so dense that light cannot escape or enter it. This, it is believed, is the source or plenum out of which this spectacular panorama is formed.

We are part of this panorama and, as some sages would tell us, at a very deep level of consciousness, we are this panorama. When we meditate, we move into that all-ness as we move beyond our individuality and touch upon our universality.

As Deepak has said many times, life is a mystery—and we are that mystery.

Week 207. Being Yourself

It seems much of our lives are spent searching for answers not only to life's deep questions, but also to what our life's work should be. Always it seems we are looking outside of ourselves, even though our answers are actually within us.

Martha Sinetar tells us we are the work we have been seeking! You are the work you've been seeking, and I am the work I've been seeking. In other words, growth and discovery are always an inside job. Through that growth, and through that discovery, our answers come.

The challenge seems to be finding your own truth so you can be your highest possible "self." Isn't that what this journey is all about?

To do that, you need to be Who You Really Are. Sometimes, just being yourself—authentically yourself—is vocation enough.

It certainly has been for me.

Week 208. Transcending our Challenges

In his book, *Walking Between the Worlds*, Gregg Braden assures us that life isn't as much about what happens to us as it is about how we use what happens. That being so, he encourages us to make conscious choices regarding the events that come into our life.

This means living life with awareness and creativity. What a powerful way to live! You see, it is in the tuning in that we find a higher path. It is in the doing that we become.

Living in a manifest world, as we all do, there is no escaping the polarities of life. When we consciously open ourselves to a higher road and walk with love in our hearts, regardless, we transcend our challenges even while moving through them.

When we can do that, everyone benefits.

Moving Through Grief

209. Finding the Gift that Adversity Brings

As unwelcome as adversity may be, it does shape and define us in ways that nothing else can. Life does have a way of presenting us with what we most need to learn when we most need to learn it. While these lessons may not come in a form we would welcome, almost always they prove to be among our most important teachers.

The good news is that nothing is ever wasted. All things do come bearing a gift, whether it seems like it at the time or not. It may take a while to find that gift, but it is there. Why is it there? Because life is always conspiring to bring the best that is possible into your life.

There will always be dark valleys to walk through. At times we may even feel there is no way out, but there is a way out. When we can go with the flow and see where life wants to take us, that way opens up for us.

When those times come, we can be sure that Wisdom is at work in our lives. This is why we can trust endings and beginnings. Trust allows a new dynamic to bring fresh meaning and purpose into our life.

For this to happen, letting go is essential. Letting go of how things were. Letting go of how we would like things to be. Letting go of the desire to change what we cannot change. Letting go is essential to our healing. Until we can truly let go, we are not free to move on with our life.

As the old saying goes, you have to put both feet in the boat before it can take you where you need to go. Letting go means putting both feet in the boat. It means accepting the lessons inherent in your situation and then moving forward on the strength of what you have learned.

Victories of the spirit require—indeed, demand—letting go of things as they were. Letting go teaches us to be comfortable with uncertainty, perhaps even learning to welcome it as a friend. True, this "simple" act of letting go is a discipline, yet its rewards are generous. Through it we learn acceptance. Acceptance allows us to see what is possible. In that understanding lies the seed of our ultimate healing.

One of the things that makes it so hard to let go of established patterns is the resistance we feel toward change. We struggle with it, perhaps even fight against it. Although this is only natural, resistance never wins. Resistance is always in a state of battle. Acceptance leads to the way out.

Acceptance allows us to see that our soul is simply changing directions. That perspective makes it easier to see what we can or cannot change. Then we are free to choose. What we choose are our thoughts, our feelings, and our response to what is happening in our life. This means going inward to where our thoughts and feelings originate. Then we align those deep inner processes with how we'd really like to live our life as we consciously join the creative process that is at work in us.

Thoughts are strange creatures. They are community-oriented critters, and they tend to multiply into more of the same. Over time, they cluster into patterns. They develop into habits. Before we know it, those habits end up governing our life. We become so accustomed to their sheer repetition that we slip into automatic. While being "on automatic" does not require much actual thinking, neither does it allow us to live our life consciously or creatively.

Being aware that we have a choice in how we think and feel is the first step toward bringing our habits into the light of conscious awareness. When we aren't on automatic, it is easier to recognize when we are being given an opportunity to learn something. If we choose to focus on that lesson, we open ourself to healthy change. This is important. When we change our response to life, our experience changes, too.

Although our challenges will all be different, there are some basic things you can do to make the going a little easier. For example, you might begin by looking at the patterns in your daily life. Pay attention to how you respond to what life is bringing your way. Listen to what you are thinking. Audit your feelings. This, in itself, is a practice. When you watch your inner activity much as an outside observer would, it is easier to see how you are molding and shaping your days. This frees you to work with the everyday events of your life and let them be your teacher, even the events that are the most difficult—especially the ones that are the most difficult. Your most difficult moments are the ones that offer you the most room for growth. Try making a conscious effort to be grateful for whatever comes into your life.

While that may sound rather simple, it is more important than you might think. Try appreciating how special each moment is. Recognize the precious opportunity inherent in each day. While you are at it, see if you can find ways to put aside some of the busy-ness that fills your days so you can reconnect with the peace and stillness that are the very ground of your being. Then bring that stillness into your daily life, into your every thought and feeling. Day after patient day, integrate that stillness and that peace into your daily living and see the difference it makes.

When you do, you may even notice there is a presence that is always with you. The faithfulness of that presence just may open a door—a way of seeing—you've never known before. You may even begin to sense that same presence in others, too. You may see that same living, loving presence looking back at you everywhere you go. Once that happens, you will know you are never really alone, no matter what. This knowledge creates a confidence and a fortitude that will help carry you through other difficult times.

Another important lesson is learning not to judge. We all do this. We judge things constantly. This is good, that is bad. This is happy, that is not. We like this, we don't like that. That kind of mindset is a form of resistance. When we judge, we aren't accepting things as they are. Whenever we resist, our inner peace is disturbed. The peace we are talking about is the peace you have found in the quiet presence of your soul.

If you find you are doing a lot of judging, it would be good to work on your thinking. At first it may seem like you are trying to catch a river, but if you stick with it, gradually—over time—you begin to notice a difference. It will get easier to let go. To let be what is. To not get hung up on results. To trust that whatever happens is for the best.

Yes, we're talking about surrender, and surrender can open up a deep source of strength when the going gets rough. You see, it really is possible to change how you meet life. It really is possible to direct your mind and teach it what you want it to do. This is important, because then you'll be able to draw a line beyond which you are not willing to go. You'll know when you are approaching deep water, and you'll consciously choose not to go where you do not want to swim. Instead, you'll focus on what you do want, so you can bring more of that quality into your experience.

Then, regardless of what else is happening in your life, you can still find some measure of happiness. You can still rest in that beautiful, loving presence you have come to know during your quiet, peaceful times. This kind of acceptance, this kind of freedom, is very healing. It allows you to use your pain as a means of growth. It allows you to see through your challenge to one of the greatest gifts it offers—who you really are.

Day after day, simply and humbly practice the truths on which you are hanging the sum total of your faith. Then you'll begin to understand that your thoughts, your life, and even your death are just stages in your journey. You'll know there is no darkness. There is only light, and it is everywhere. More and more, you'll begin to see that the fabric of your life is one uncut, unbroken whole. More than that, you'll know that you are whole, regardless of what else may be going on. This is the ultimate healing. In that moment of silent understanding, all your fears just slip away as quietly as they came.

210. The Early Stages of Grief

It is so easy to feel overwhelmed after the loss of a loved one. Routines have changed. Responsibilities have changed. Everything seems so different. While it is true that nothing will ever be the same again, life does continue.

Working through grief broadens your vision as you learn that life and love do not end. While it is true that the physical body does not last forever, the relationship you had has not ended. The love continues.

In the meantime, there is much you can do to help yourself move through this new chapter of your life. It is particularly important, at this fragile time, to nourish yourself on every level—physically, mentally, emotionally, and yes, spiritually. Healing from a wound like this doesn't happen all at once, so take things a day at a time. When that seems like too much, just get through this hour, this minute. To help you do that, here are some suggestions that can help ease the stress and grief you are feeling. Find the ones that speak to you the most, and start there.

1. Make sure you're getting the rest you need. This may mean taking a break from whatever you're doing to nap or just relax. Even stopping for a cup of calming tea or taking a leisurely walk can work wonders.
2. At times like this, forgetting things is normal. It just means your "circuits" are on overload. If this is happening to you, make lists. Do short tasks that don't require long periods of concentration. If you keep forgetting appointments, ask someone to remind

you. This, too, will pass. It just takes time for all of the parts of your system to re-set themselves, so be patient with yourself. It will get better, I promise.

3. Avoid hasty decisions. Put off major decisions until you are ready to face them.

4. Cry whenever you need to. Tears provide a healthy release and help clear out the cobwebs.

5. Don't hesitate to talk about your feelings with others, particularly someone you are comfortable with.

6. Spend time with others, whether you feel like it or not.

7. Consider starting a journal where you can reflect on what happened and how this has changed your life. A journal lets you release pent-up feelings and helps you begin the healing process. Just a few minutes a day gives you a framework from which you can view the changes you are going through.

8. Make sure some form of exercise is part of your daily routine. It doesn't have to be anything strenuous. Stretching or a few easy yoga poses can ease whatever tensions you might be feeling. Even something as simple as a 20-minute walk can lift your spirit. Choose an activity you enjoy, one you can look forward to.

9. Ask for help when you need it, whether that means getting something from the top shelf or a more complicated task, like making changes to your insurance. On a deeper level, don't hesitate to talk with someone when you're feeling down and need help sorting things out.

10. Eating small meals 4-5 times a day helps curb emotional swings by keeping your blood sugar on an even keel.

11. Make sure you drink a lot of water. I'm talking about 8-10 glasses a day. Every cell is dependent on water. A dehydrated body doesn't function well and pulls you down emotionally. A hydrated body is a happy body, and a happy body ... well, you get the idea.

12. Also make sure you breathe deeply, at least some of the time. The body gets the oxygen it needs from the bottom of the lungs. When we are tense and feeling stressed, our breathing tends to be shallow. Insufficient oxygen stresses the body and adds to the stress you are already feeling. Conscious slow, deep breathing not only helps you relax, it gives your system the oxygen it requires to function normally. If you're finding it difficult to breathe deeply, try breathing in and out through an imaginary straw to help the oxygen get to the bottom of your lungs.

Another excellent technique is to raise your arms slowly while breathing in through your nose, gauging the intake so you reach capacity when the arms are all the way up. Then slowly exhale on "sssss" while slowly lowering the arms, again gauging your movement so you reach "empty" when the arms are all the way down. Repeat this 2 or 3 times and then stop and smile. Do this several times a day, or whenever you're feeling particularly stressed.

13. Listen to your body and trust its wisdom! The body never lies. Its signals are either comfort or discomfort or, as Author Tom Robbins would say, "yuk or yum."

14. Spend some time each day praying or meditating. These practices bring you back to your peaceful center and help restore a sense of stability in your life.

15. Read something uplifting every day.

16. Put positive statements around the house where you can see them.

17. Listen to beautiful music. Music takes you where the mind cannot go.

18. Don't forget about humor. Deliberately find something to laugh about each day. Even though laughing may be the last thing you feel like doing, do it anyway. Give yourself permission to laugh about something. Laughter breaks up the clouds and leaves you in a better place.

19. Do at least one thing you enjoy every day.

20. Try to end each day giving thanks for your blessings. Even in the toughest of times, there is still something for which you can be thankful. What can you give thanks for today? Did support come from an unexpected place? Did someone say exactly what you needed to hear? Did a robin stop and sing on your window sill? Blessings come in many forms. You may even wish to begin a gratitude journal in which you record how each day blessed you. Gratitude heals at very deep levels.

21. Try going to bed around the same time every night. A regular routine helps create a feeling of stability. If sleep is difficult for you, a soothing bath or a cup of chamomile tea early in the evening will help you settle down as you prepare for sleep.

22. Go at your own pace. Grief doesn't have a time table. Allow yourself to do what you need to do and feel what you need to feel in order to heal. You are doing the very best you can at any given time, so be easy on yourself and let the process unfold.

No matter how difficult things may seem, there is always a way. You are being guided, whether it seems like it or not. Trust in that Wisdom. It knows the way.

211. Restoring Balance

There are many facets to grief. There are many stages, too. Grief is complex. It touches every level of your being. All the more reason to pay attention to those levels when grief has entered your life. I wish I had known that when my husband died so suddenly. I thought I should just keep going, regardless. So I did. Until I was on the verge of collapse.

Sometimes we push ourself until our system makes it clear that our body is going to be in trouble—big trouble—if we don't stop and pay attention to what it needs. That is what happened to me. How much better it would be if we could just stop and say, "Ok, the focus has shifted here. I really do need to take care of myself and listen to what my system is telling me," and then do just that. Believe me, it is the smartest thing you'll ever do. Until you listen—really listen—you'll never know what you need to do to get back in balance.

212. Unending Love

One of the things that makes it difficult to adjust after losing our loved ones is the absence of their physical presence. While there is no denying that we cannot see them anymore, the love is still there. That love is a link that cannot be broken. One could even say that love is our eternal connection to each other. Love joins us in spirit, whether we can see each other or not.

Some of my children live 1,500 miles from me, yet we are very close. Our love for each other connects us every day and makes their presence feel very real.

It is no different for those who are no longer with us physically. Once we can no longer enjoy their physical presence, we become even more aware of the love we shared and how it is still very much a part of us. It is as though our love has expanded and taken on a deeper dimension. Indeed it has, for love is the very essence of our being.

Love is our very nature. It is the fabric of who and what we are. As our awareness of that loving presence increases, we begin to realize that we can never be separated, for we are all expressions of the one infinite, loving Spirit.

When we begin to truly "get" that, we find great comfort in the knowledge that the love we shared lives on. It is there to support and sustain us in ways we may not have imagined before.

The death of a loved one brings many lessons, but it also carries with it great gifts. The realization of this unending love is one of those gifts.

213. From Loneliness to Solitude

Perhaps one of the most difficult aspects of losing a loved one is the feeling of having been left alone. The loss of the presence, the personality, the person with whom we had blended so well leaves an acute sense of loneliness. It is easy to feel lost, abandoned even, with no idea of where to go. All sense of purpose seems to have evaporated. We feel very much like a ship without a rudder, and the seas do not feel like friendly seas at all. It is hard to keep going, to even try at times like these. Yet we know we must, and so we do, hoping that one day we will be able to make sense out of it all.

While loneliness can seem formidable, it is not inescapable, and it can indeed become our friend. Being alone gives us the time we need to get in touch with ourself. To listen to our deep needs. To nourish our soul. Being alone provides the space we need to find the route that goes within where we can hear the things that can only be heard in the deep silence of our soul.

Loneliness is a fertile arena for growth, for introspection, for reflection. There is no denying our attention has been captured. Whether we like it or not, this is new territory. Explore it we must, for that is the only way out. So we begin, hesitantly, a step at a time, climbing, stumbling, perhaps even falling. As we move through this new terrain, we discover—step by hesitant step—new vistas, new meanings, new purpose in life.

Along the way, we may find ourself weighing things which perhaps we have not thought about for a long time. What is it that really matters? What is it that gives meaning and purpose to our life? Where can we find hope for the future, or even the desire to go on? These are all things we ponder as we try to gain a toehold on the mountain we now must climb.

Change does force us to look at life through a different prism. When it does, priorities get rearranged. What we thought was important before may not seem to matter now at all, while things we may not have thought about for a long time loom quite large in front of us. It's a balancing process really, weighing this against that as we seek to find what rings true within us. Even our beliefs may change. What we had thought before may not seem quite so in these new surroundings. The nature of our reality has taken on new proportions. Our insight does, too, bringing us to new horizons which we feel impelled to explore. It is very much an interior process, a spiritual journey that can lead us into the deepest part of our being.

Yes, this may be the winter of our soul. Even though all may seem barren and empty, it is very much a fertile time, a time of preparation, a seed-planting time in the inner recesses of our being. As we enter into the process of self-discovery, new ideas and new concepts begin to surface. New insights beckon from some distant horizon. Gradually, we find ourself letting go of the past as we enter into this new season of our lives.

In coming to understand ourself better, we begin to understand others better also. We become more aware of their pain, their sorrow, their grief. We sense more clearly our shared humanity, our common goals and dreams. As this awareness grows, our desire to reach out does, too. Their pain becomes our pain even as their joy is our joy. It is then we find we were never really alone. It only seemed so. Our sense of connection has changed, but it has not grown less. It has become more. It has broadened. Through the very nature of our struggle, it has also become enriched.

True, things will never be the same, nor would we have come this way by choice. Yet having found ourself in this new place, this growing place, over the passage of time we begin to make friends with it. The space with which we once struggled, which once seemed so empty, becomes for us an arena of possibility, a place where potential can be explored. It affords us a time to rest, to heal, to renew ourself as we prepare for whatever direction our journey now must take.

In the process, our transformation begins. Without our even knowing it, subtle changes occur within us. Our sense of identity becomes clearer. As the emotional fog we have been in begins to lift, a new sense of direction begins to appear. Gradually the loneliness, the emptiness which once seemed so acute becomes transformed. The quiet becomes a haven. The silence becomes our sanctuary. We begin to welcome the times when we can retreat from all that is in the outer and simply rest in the peace we have learned to find within us.

Solitude becomes the gift that springs from seeds of loneliness. It grows in the fertile soil that grief creates. It is the beginning of a new way of life as we embrace a clearer sense of identity, a broader sense of purpose, a deeper sense of connection with all people. Now we know that while forms may change, life itself does not end. Even though separation may seem to have occurred, relationships are still intact. All is not lost, only changed.

Over time, if we are patient, our loneliness changes into a healing space. As it does, we discover the answers we have been seeking are actually within us. They are the truth of our being, kept safely for us in our deepest heart of hearts. They reveal themselves to us through the peace, the love, the presence, and yes, even the joy we find as we return time and again to the sanctuary of our soul.

214. Solitude's Transforming Power

Solitude opens the door to a deeper, more complete way of being. While that thought may not feel very comforting, it is through solitude that we find the peace—and yes, the joy—we are seeking. As we befriend our quiet inner times, we become more at home with ourself. We find inner strengths we may not have known were there. We find another way of being where we feel more connected with ourself, more whole.

Whether we know it or not, even whether we will admit it or not, solitude does feed our soul. In solitude we get in touch with our deepest thoughts and feelings. In solitude we find out what's going on inside us. Until we've done that, how can we know where we are going, or even where we want to go?

Truly, embracing solitude is a gift you can give yourself—a gift that allows you to be with yourself, to really get to know and appreciate yourself, so you can really be what you are capable of being. In being That, you satisfy your own deep longings.

Where else are you going to find the answers you long for if it isn't within yourself? Oh yes, you can look to others for answers, but when you do, isn't it more for confirmation of what you already inwardly sense to be true?

Radical change forces us to stop and take stock of our situation. We may even find ourself asking, "Where do I go from here?" The answer is waiting for you in your heart. When you listen to what your heart is saying, you will find both a purpose and a sense of direction for this new time in your life. You will find the "something" that brings new meaning to your days.

There is no denying that times of change are stretching, learning, growing times. As we expand in awareness of our nature and our potential, we may feel somewhat uneasy with the promise of unlimited growth. How can we be ready to be more when we are not yet comfortable with what we are now? It is a question that has no answer, but perhaps it does not need one. The process is a gradual one, so subtle that it happens without our even knowing it. We might just as well try to watch the grass grow, but grow it does—and so do we—in just the right way, at just the right time.

In some ways I think the caterpillar is wiser than we are, for it knows when the time has come to build its cocoon and enter into the process of change. We are not such willing creatures, by and large. Perhaps it is because the change was so unwelcome. Yet, if we were to prepare ourself, if we were to admit that someday this time of transition will also be ours to make, perhaps we would be more open to its lessons. Perhaps the very act of accepting things for what they are would allow us to enter into this time of change in a more graceful way.

It is a birthing process really, a becoming so interior in its occurrence that only in the silence can it creep into our awareness. Indeed, were we not looking we would never know it was there, but it is there. This is the stuff of life that molds and shapes us and brings a new dynamic into our experience. That dynamic gives us both meaning and purpose as we encounter the truths we have been seeking.

In that birthing, subtle and sometimes unseen, is the undeniable need to let go. Only when we do can the miracle truly happen.

215. Reflections on Letting Go

Grief creeps into our lives in so many ways. Loved ones die, friends or family move away, children grow up and leave home, jobs change, pets die, a treasured possession becomes damaged or lost. These are just some of the things we must cope with as we move through our days. Such changes are links to the past, to what we know and are comfortable with. Being creatures who prefer comfort, we do not readily welcome change. The past—the "known"—has become our friend. Yet it is only in the present that our truest joys can be found. It is only in this moment that we can most fully experience the peaks—and yes, the valleys—of life.

If this is true, then why do we find it so difficult to be here—now? Perhaps it is simply a matter of habit. Are we programmed to walk through life with our head on backwards, looking at where we have been? That is what grief is, you know—a backwards glance.

As I sit here working on my computer—my word processor—it occurs to me that perhaps we are experience processors. We must be if we are ever to make sense out of—or find the meaning and value in—our experiences. The key is not to get stuck there. Once we have made our evaluation, once we have made peace with an issue, we must be willing to let go. We must be willing to move on.

There are many things that challenge us to do this, not the least of which is the loss of a loved one. Eventually, we even have to let go of life as we knew it. We must be willing to let the river take us where it will, whether we know our destination or not. While this is not necessarily an easy thing to do, it is possible.

Letting go of how things were. Letting go of how we would like things to be. Letting go of the need to try to change what we cannot change. Letting go implies a willingness to give up the old and embrace the new. Yes, letting go is incremental to our healing. Until we can let go, we cannot move forward. As I have often said, you have to put both feet in the boat before it can take you where you need to go. Letting go means accepting the lessons inherent in your situation and then moving forward on the strength of what you have learned. It means knowing what you can control and what you can't, and then being at peace with that knowledge.

How are such victories won? Certainly not by clinging to the past. Not by hanging on to what cannot be changed. No, victories of the spirit require—indeed, demand—letting go of things as they were. When you do, it makes all the difference.

When I was in the throes of grief, there came a time when I began to wonder if clinging so tightly to my deceased husband was holding him back, wherever he was. I certainly didn't want to do that, so I made the conscious decision to let him go. When I did, I was astonished to find that he wanted the very same thing for me! It was an amazing moment, filled with the joy of knowing that now we were both free to go on with our lives, him wherever he was, and me where I am. I cannot imagine a deeper love than the love I felt when we gave each other that precious gift.

I think we have to get to a certain point in our healing before we are strong enough to be able to let go like that, but when we do, its rewards are generous. Through it we find that place within ourself where we can accept what has happened. Through that acceptance, we find the strength to start moving forward with our life. Therein lies the beginning of the deep healing of our spirit. That healing brings a sense of freedom, a joy beyond description, and yes, a peace that surpasses by far all the sorrow we have ever known.

216. Choosing to Be Happy

Life is full of choices, including the choice to be happy. While it may seem strange to think of being happy as a choice, that is one of the lessons life presents us when we are working through loss.

That lesson presented itself to me about eight months after my husband's sudden death. We had planned to visit our dear friends down in Florida, so I got up my courage and went by myself in the early part of the year. While I was there, they decided to have a Super Bowl party. It was also my host's birthday, which meant there were a lot of people and a lot of laughter. The laughter really troubled me. I didn't see how everyone could be having such a good time when I was in such awful pain.

It was then I realized that the sadness I felt so keenly belonged to me. It was my own personal experience. The only way that feeling was going to change was if I changed, but to be "happy," to laugh—to really laugh—felt dishonest. When I tried to laugh, it felt like I was denying the importance of my husband's passing. I knew he didn't want me to spend the rest of my life crying. What to do? I was stuck, and I knew it.

I thought about that a lot over the next few days. Finally I decided to just give myself permission to be happy. It wasn't the same happy I had known before, and it certainly wasn't the happy I know now, but it was a start. It was a place to begin.

I think that is how it is for many of us. We have to give ourself permission to not work so hard, to be kind to ourself, even to nurture ourself, and yes, to follow the deep calling in our heart that can lead us to the happiness we are seeking. Once we make that choice, our healing is assured.

217. Laughter's Blessings

Soon after my return home from Florida, something happened that caused me to laugh—I mean, *really* laugh. I was surprised at how good it felt. It also surprised me when I thought about how long it had been since I had last laughed. I decided then and there that I would start laughing, even if I had to make a conscious decision to do it. But how to get started?

As I thought about it, I knew we had books and magazines with something funny in them, so I started raiding the bookshelves, pulling out anything and everything that might trigger some laughter, and I put it all on the dining room table. From that point forward, I read something after each meal, determined not to get up until I had had a good laugh.

I was amazed at how much the laughter helped. Since that time I have learned that laughter is one of nature's most natural and most healing mechanisms, not just for grief but for many illnesses, too.

The reason for this is simple. Our state of mind is connected to our breathing. Usually when we are feeling stressed, our breathing is shallow, but the body gets the oxygen it needs from the bottom of the lungs, not the top. That is just one of the reasons why laughter is so effective.

Laughter engages the diaphragm which is connected to the bottom of the lungs. When we move the diaphragm, we pull oxygen into the bottom of the lungs, thereby releasing some of the stress we are feeling—physically, mentally, and emotionally. In fact, 10 minutes of deep, healthy laughter is equal to 30 minutes of aerobic activity! That is why laughter gets those spirit-lifting endorphins going. And if you're experiencing physical pain for whatever reason, 30 minutes of belly laughter can give you two hours of pain relief! Just another reason to bring laughter into your day!

What if it's just too hard for you to laugh right now? Then begin doing some deep breathing. Yoga teaches some excellent pranayamas (breathing exercises) which are very effective. If you don't practice yoga or can't get to a class, just start breathing deeply on purpose. It doesn't have to be for a long time. Even 5 or 10 deep breaths repeated throughout your day will make a difference.

There are other things you can do to lighten up, too. Here are just a few:

- Smile.
- Count your blessings.
- When you hear laughter, move toward it.
- Spend time with happy, playful people.
- Bring humor into conversations.
- Laugh at yourself.
- Try to laugh at stressful situations rather than bemoaning them.
- Take charge of your thoughts, emotions, environment, and the way you deal with problems.
- Surround yourself with reminders to lighten up. Keep things in perspective.
- Deal with your stress.
- Pay attention to children and emulate them.
- Find a laughter group in your area and join it.
- Make it a habit to start and end your day with laughter.
- Start laughing every chance you can, even if you have to fake it.
- Laughter does make a difference. I promise.

218. Two Sides of the Coin

Moments of crisis have a way of bringing our focus into stark relief. They get our attention. They force us to plumb our spiritual depths. They put on the brakes and make us look at what life is really all about.

Perhaps it is not this way for everyone, but that is how it has been for me. My "spiritual life" and my "working life" have always walked hand in hand. Even though there were times when one was more in the forefront than the other, they have been like two sides of a coin.

My husband's sudden passing changed everything. My spiritual hunger became the heavy end of the scale. It demanded my attention. It forced me to search my depths for what I needed.

Painful as it was, those times became immensely productive and fruitful. Thus, challenge became my friend. If ever I needed it, here was proof that all things do indeed come bearing a gift, if we will but look for it. The gift, then, was the growth I made, the inner blossoming that occurred as I worked my way through the pain and heartache into the sunlight that was patiently waiting for me on the other side of my darkness.

Thus it was that even my most unwelcome challenge brought answers I'd been seeking all of my life. That is why I believe this is possible for all of us. Simple questions like "What can I learn from this?" create an open mind and an open heart. That posture allows us to receive answers that ease our pain. It gives us the strength and courage to go on with our life—not as victims, but as conquerors who found a way to triumph, even in life's most difficult circumstances.

219. Special Occasions

I will never forget how hard it was to get through all of the special occasions after my husband died. There were just so many "firsts," whether it was Thanksgiving, Christmas, new babies being born, Memorial Day, and yes, all of those birthdays. Whatever the occasion was, it was hard. What I learned was you just have to do what you need to do to get yourself through it.

For example, it had been our tradition on Memorial Day to drive 50 miles away to the cemetery where my husband's family graves were. We did that every single year, rain or shine, but on that first Memorial Day after his passing, I just couldn't do it. My solution was to leave town and visit my son in Georgia. That was my excuse for not being there when they had the 21-gun salute and played taps at the cemetery. I was there in my heart, but on that particular holiday the only way I could deal with it was by being 1,500 miles away.

Little by little, I began to understand that it is all right to do whatever is necessary to get through those difficult occasions. It's part of the healing process, part of learning to accept what is, what we cannot change. How we do that will be different for all of us. There is no right or wrong. The only constant is we always have a choice in how we do it, and that is as it should be.

It's been over twenty-five years now since Neal's passing, and almost that long since I lost my parents. I've "picked up the pieces and moved on," as the old expression goes. Even now, when I think I've "dealt with it," every great once in a while something comes along and the floodgate opens. I don't know if we ever truly "bring closure" to such a loss. This much I can promise—eventually we do reach the point where our loss becomes less consuming and we are able to move on more easily with our life.

220. When Life Gets Turned Upside Down

Life is very much a continual weaning process. We come into the world dependent on other people. Over the course of time we are forced more and more to rely not as much on others as on That which is both our Source and Sustainer. I'm talking about learning to put your hand in the only Hand that can lead you not only through life but through death as well.

The process begins when death first comes into our lives as children through the gradual loss of family and friends. It does not end until we, too, face the portal which only the soul can enter. How we deal with these losses, how we let our faith sustain us, how we allow that Hand to lead us, no matter what, determines how we approach that door.

It is said that children learn through watching. I think we all do. In seeing how others cope with the challenge grief presents, we each are forced to weigh our own beliefs and attitudes. We are challenged to search out what rings true in our deepest heart of hearts as we continue developing the premise on which we are trying to build our foundation.

There is considerable responsibility here, when you stop and think about it. Accepting the inevitable and making peace with it enables you to find a Way when there does not seem to be a way. It allows you to reach for the heights even while your spirit is at the depths of its grief.

Acceptance makes it possible not only for you to go on, to find new meaning and new purpose for your life, but to do it knowing that all is not lost, only changed. While that change can be soul-shattering, strength is forged from the crucible of your grief even while joy is found in the knowledge that this is not the end but rather a beginning.

Yes, it is the beginning of a new chapter in which we learn that the relationships that helped make us what we are have not ended at all. Indeed, they have become richer through this new dimension in which they now must find expression. Now we see that the cycles which may seem to separate us are but the cycles of our evolution. As we seek, through faith, the means and the will to continue, so, too, do we find new meaning and purpose for our life. It is this meaning and this purpose that enables us to face death, even our own death, with a serenity and a peace that is born of the knowledge that all is well—and all shall be well—even when life has been turned upside down and all is changed beyond recognition.

221. Love Never Ends

There were so many "firsts" after losing my husband and both parents, but the one thing that was constant through all of that was the sense of their loving presence. It just felt as though they were still here. That came as a complete surprise to me. I really thought they were gone, but they weren't gone. Not entirely. We were still connected through our love. That was when I began to understand that relationships change, but they do not end. They cannot end, because love never ends. Love cannot die. Love is eternal. That eternal love is at the very heart of our being.

This new perspective made it easier to let go of the pain that grief wants to impose. Eventually I realized I did not need the pain any longer. It became a hindrance and so, as much as was possible, I let it go. Surprisingly, that is when the "miracle" happened, for in that letting go I was allowed to see what I still have—indeed, what I never lost at all. The wonderful, indescribable, nurturing love we shared seemed to have expanded and resolved into a presence that now is a constant part of my awareness.

In changing form, our relationships became even more. It seemed to be saying that the love we shared was just the beginning, that the best was yet to come, and all that followed would be an expansion of that love.

Time has proven that to be true. The connection—and the love—were never broken. Finding that out deepened my understanding and enriched my life, making it possible for me to go forward in peace.

222. Where to Go from Here

Even though I'd heard the expression, "Whenever a door closes, a window always opens," I didn't see how that could apply to my life. I was feeling so lost, with no sense of direction. Not knowing what else to do, I started asking, "What do You want me to do now, Lord?" and I asked that question repeatedly.

Gradually, without my ever knowing how, a whole new life opened up for me, a life filled with meaning, purpose, and a deep sense of contentment and joy. I'm not talking about the "happy" that comes when we "get" something, or when something nice happens. I'm talking about the joy of following your spiritual path and growing into a deeper, more authentic expression of who you really are.

If you are wondering what to do next, my suggestion would be to start asking, "Where do You want me to go from here?" God never ignores an open heart.

223. Re-Claiming Joy

Re-claiming joy is an inward journey, one that requires a willingness to let go of our pain, and yes, even the narrow confines of our thinking.

We are so much more than we know. To move beyond our boundaries and scale the heights within us requires a dedication and a passion to explore the unknown territory of our soul. It is there—on the heights within us—that we can re-claim not only our joy, but a love beyond anything we have yet imagined, a love that radiates outward through our wholeness, not our woundedness.

I'm talking about a love that is born out of our connection with our Source. When we find that sacred link within us, we begin to understand what has been hidden from us all this time—that we are the love and the joy we have been seeking.

224. The Paradox of Great Change

When great change comes into our lives, we may feel as though we are in a foreign land. All seems different somehow, and we may feel hesitant or unsure as to how to proceed. To be sure, a door has opened before us, a door that perhaps we may not wish to go through, and yet we must proceed in one way or another. Life does go on, and so must we.

The question, then, becomes "How do we proceed?" Always we have a choice. Much depends on how we exercise that prerogative.

Change can be an unwanted guest, and we its reluctant companion. Of this much we can be certain—it does force our hand. It gets us out of our rut. It causes us to re-think our situation, to look for new ways of doing things. Whether we like it or not, change is a part of life that must be dealt with.

It is hard to say why life's lessons often come in such an unwelcome form. Speaking for myself, I have to admit that, had the struggle not been pressed upon me, I would not have chosen to face the issues and deal with the challenges that have brought me to where I am.

Therein lies the paradox, for unwelcome as change can sometimes be, it can prove to be a friend in disguise, an unexpected ally that, through its very presence, causes us to reach further than we have reached before. It motivates us to strengthen the weak places, to overcome the hard spots, to transcend that which we felt unable to face.

I have often wondered if change brings about a form of inner aerobics, for through it we do develop our spiritual sinews as we find a way to go forward. Challenge can be daunting. One must be willing to be a spiritual explorer to venture into the unknown, and yet—how else are we to get there?

I often think of the explorers in the early days of our country, reaching for horizon after horizon as the vast expanse of the plains and mountains, desert and highlands all unfolded before them, one difficult step after another. What courage it must have taken for them to journey forth in such a fashion.

Is that any different from what we do every day when we work through the challenges that mold and shape our lives? Great horizons wait before us, too. Adventures we have not as yet even thought of lie just around the bend. Potential beyond our greatest dreams awaits those who are willing to follow their inner leading and move into the unknown regions of their soul where they might discover the very secrets of existence within themselves.

We all are searching for meaning in our lives. We all hope to find the courage to meet our tests and trials, but the qualities that get us through the rough spots can never be developed without the inner exercise it takes to strengthen them.

As with any endeavor, ability only comes with practice. That is what we're doing every day of our lives. We're developing our inner skills. We're clarifying our identity. We're reaching for some illusive, undefined goal that keeps urging us on with no hint of what our destination might be.

Perhaps that's how it's supposed to be. Perhaps it's the mystery and intrigue that keep egging us on, that whet our appetite and make us want to continue our climb. We can only trust that there is a purpose behind the chaos, a reason behind the struggle.

Perhaps that purpose goes deeper than we think. Perhaps there is Something inside us that is nudging us on, that is planting the desire within us to grow, to expand our boundaries, to become more than we yet are. Certainly the call is there. Its voice can be heard in every challenge that confronts us. How we respond to that voice will be different for each of us, but respond we must, one way or another.

We would do well to view our challenges much as mountain climbers view the mountain. They climb it because it's there. So must we as we work through our difficulties. We adjust and we grow.

Life is growth. Life is change. If we can look at this aspect of our daily existence as new territory to explore, as a new world that is opening to us, perhaps we, too, will end up stronger than we were before—enriched inwardly and outwardly by the very knowledge that the mountain was there, and we climbed it.

Index

Please Note: These numbers indicate the Weeks in which the Subject appears and not the page number

About The Author

Donna's spiritual path led to extensive work with some of today's premier teachers of spirituality. She studied with Dr. Deepak Chopra for twenty-five years and is one of Chopra Global's certified meditation and yoga instructors. She achieved the level of Quantum Explorer in Remote Viewing after training with Dr. David Morehouse. She also completed the advanced level of intensive training in Sound Healing with Jonathan Goldman, and has studied with Roger Gabriel both in the United States and in India. The teachings of Dr. David Hawkins also had a profound influence on her writing and teaching. Add to this the many other authors whose works Donna studied and you have the rich source of Wisdom that inspired her teaching and writing.

For the past 35 years, Donna Miesbach's award-winning poems and articles have spanned the globe through such venues as *Daily Word, Unity Magazine, Christian Living in the Mature Years, Contemplative Journal,* and the *Chicken Soup* Series. It is with a deep sense of gratitude that Ms. Miesbach offers this collection from her "Thought for the Week" series which she began over 20 years ago.

Made in the USA
Middletown, DE
21 April 2022

64429855R10104